# SWEET JESUS

# SWEET JESUS

## POEMS ABOUT THE ULTIMATE ICON

EDITED AND WITH AN INTRODUCTION BY
NICK CARBÓ AND DENISE DUHAMEL

WITH A FOREWORD BY
DAN WAKEFIELD

[**anthology** press]
Los Angeles, California

Anthology Press
P.O. Box 291339, Los Angeles, California 90029

Distributed in the U.S. by Small Press Distribution
Printed in the United States of America

First edition, 2002
Library of Congress Control Number: 2002106603
ISBN 0-9720559-0-8

Book design by Robert Kranzke
Cover design by David Hernandez and Robert Kranzke
Cover photograph by Patrick Pardo

Credits and acknowledgments for the poems in this book appear on page 187.

# CONTENTS

## JESUS IS JUST ALRIGHT

## APOCRYPHAL JESUS

## CONTEMPORARY JESUS

# Foreword | By Dan Wakefield

As a hot-shot collegiate atheist at Columbia University back in the nineteen fifties, I would never have deigned to read anything about Jesus if the Gospels hadn't been included in a course called "The Narrative Art," created and taught by the Pulitzer Prize–winning poet Mark Van Doren. This legendary teacher, who influenced generations of writers from Thomas Merton to Allen Ginsberg, shattered my childhood (and childish) image of Jesus one morning in the classroom when he lectured on The New Testament—not as religion but as literature.

"Many of you have an idea from Sunday School that Jesus was some kind of wispy character floating around Jerusalem in a night shirt," Van Doren said. "But this is not true. Jesus was the most ruthless of men."

Whoa!

Through Van Doren *the poet*'s perception, I began to see Jesus as—whatever else he might have been—a fascinating character.

For more than 2,000 years now, beginning with Matthew, Mark, Luke and John, writers have found—and as this book demonstrates, continue to find—Jesus to be an immensely compelling subject. Whether Christian, Jew, atheist or agnostic, whether viewing Jesus with awe or anger, lovingly or comically, sardonically or sweetly, in song or story, novel or drama, prose or poetry, writers persist in exploring Jesus as subject matter.

What a great idea of the poets Nick Carbó and Denise Duhamel to collect into one book an exciting array of contemporary poems on this age-old and yet always-new subject. Jesus is made fresh, renewed—even "born again," you might say—with every successive generation of writers. How fitting that the work of poets in particular has been assembled to reflect the image of Jesus in today's vernacular. Jesus' own parables were poems, as was his own brief, luminous life—a story, as the poet and novelist Reynolds Price put it, "to compel the fascination of a huge majority of the human race ever afterward."

What finally amazes here is not that there are so many current poems about Jesus, or that they are so dazzlingly diverse in style, viewpoint and sentiment, but that they share such a sense of vibrant life—not just liveliness but being alive—living, now.

Dan Wakefield's books include *Returning: A Spiritual Journey, Creating from the Spirit, The Story of Your Life: Writing a Spiritual Autobiography, Expect a Miracle* and *How Do We Know When It's God?: A Spiritual Memoir.* He is a novelist, journalist and screenwriter whose best-selling novels *Going All the Way* and *Starting Over* were produced as feature films. In addition, he created the NBC prime time TV series *James at 15*, and his memoir, *New York in the Fifties*, was produced as a documentary film.

# Introduction | By Nick Carbó and Denise Duhamel

SOME THIRTY YEARS AGO, John Lennon proclaimed that the Beatles were "bigger than Christ." Little did he know what would follow: the movies *Jesus Christ Superstar* and *The Last Temptation of Christ*; pop hits like fellow Beatle George Harrison's "My Sweet Lord," The Doobie Brothers' "Jesus Is Just Alright," George Michael's "Jesus to a Child," and, more recently, alternative-music songs such as Depeche Mode's "Personal Jesus," My Life with the Thrill Kill Cult's "Kooler Than Jesus," Ministry's "Jesus Built My Hot Rod," Greg Brown's "Jesus and Elvis," King Missile's "Jesus Was Way Cool" and Tom Waits' "Chocolate Jesus." Currently, the word "Jesus" appears in the titles of 1,793 available pop and rock songs according to Barnes & Noble's Muze electronic music schedule. In addition to Jesus Jones, musical performers have adopted such names as The Jesus & Mary Chain, Teenage Jesus and the Jerks, Jesus Christ Superfly, Liquid Jesus, Acid Jesus, The Jesus Lizard, and March for Jesus.

The February 1996 issue of *Spin Magazine* goes as far as to declare, through an elaborate chart with mini-guitar and mini-church icons, that Jesus is back on top, popularity-wise, no longer threatened by the British invasion. Though Jesus' commercial success as the "protagonist of the world's best-selling book" can't match the Beatles' as the "world's best-selling band," Jesus *does* have the advantage in several other important areas. For example, Jesus clearly has the catchier nickname ("The Son of God" vs. "The Fab Four"), the more coveted artifact ("the Shroud of Turin" vs. "bedsheets from the Fontainbleu Hotel"), and is the performer of the more miraculous miracle ("turning water into wine" vs. "driving Pat Boone off the radio").

Inspired by Lucinda Ebersole and Rick Peabody's poetry anthologies *Mondo Barbie, Mondo Elvis, Mondo Marilyn* and *Mondo James Dean*, we began to think that surely Jesus deserved a collection of poems about Him, too. Not another devotional poetry book—there are enough of those already—but a book that explores Jesus as the cultural icon that He is. Ever since Madonna made the rosary a fashion statement, Jesus has surely been "in" with the in crowd, and He has over the years inspired a rash of imitators. Long hair on men is forever coming back into style, and it doesn't take an astute observer of footwear to notice that Birkenstocks seem modeled on Jesus' very own sandals. The December 1995 *Harper's* Index noted that there are six California driver's licenses made out to Jesus Christ and one made out to Jesus Christ II.

Of course, Jesus has always been a subject for writers, since the days of the storytellers and poets who authored the Bible within sixty-five years of Jesus' death. Later, there were the medieval mystery plays, and George Moore's *The Brook Kerith*, Nikos Kazantzakis' *The Last Temptation of Christ*, D.H. Lawrence's short story "The Man Who Died," A.J. Langguth's *Jesus Christs*, Anthony Burgess' *Man of Nazareth* and Romulus Linney's collection of short stories *Jesus Tales*. Michael Moorcock's *Behold the Man*, a 1960's sci-fi classic, employs Jesus as the main character. At present, there are over 100 books in print with "Jesus" in the title; many are books of religious instruction, but others prefer a more sociological take on their subject, with titles such as *Jesus Acted Up: A Gay and Lesbian Manifesto* by Robert Goss, *The Illegitimacy of Jesus: A*

*Feminist Theological Interpretation of the Infancy Narratives* by Jane Schaberg and *Women and Jesus in Mark: A Japanese Feminist Perspective* by Hisako Kinukawa.

In his memoir, *A Different Person*, the late poet James Merrill explained his admiration for Jesus through a clever series of comparisons with writers whom he revered: "Like Baudelaire he had a weakness for loose women. Like Mallarmé he enthralled and mystified his disciples; like Oscar Wilde, courted ruin at the height of his fame. Like Proust he had dipped, with miraculous consequences, a cookie into a restorative cup..."

Because Jesus is part of the Trinity, we technically could have included many great poems about The Father and The Holy Ghost as well (poems that followed in the tradition of John Donne's poem "Batter My Heart"). Instead, our focus was on poetry about Jesus the man. We tried to include poems that would somehow challenge the traditional notion of Jesus, bring Him up to date and give Him a new wardrobe and new vocabulary.

When we began to solicit poets for *Sweet Jesus*, we weren't sure exactly what we would get in return, though we were hoping for the irreverently reverent or the reverently irreverent. So we were delighted when we began to receive letters and homoerotic poems from "believers" such as Timothy Liu and David A. Neal, Jr., as well as poems musing about the sex life of Jesus, from Dorianne Laux and Catie Rosemurgy.

We have divided the anthology into four sections: *Strange Faith* ("spiritual" Jesus poems), *Jesus Is Just Alright* (Jesus poems from non-Christian perspectives), *Apocryphal Jesus* (poems that attempt to fill in the missing holes of Bible stories) and *Contemporary Jesus* (poems that imagine what it would be like for Jesus today should He return anytime soon). Even the unrepentantly hip cannot help but ponder the predictions of Nostradamus, zealous preachers and tabloid astrologers. A popular T-shirt slogan a few summers ago in New York City's Greenwich Village read "JESUS IS COMING—LOOK BUSY."

It would be naive of us, and the contributors, to ignore the conservative political climate of our present-day United States. In 1995, the National Endowment for the Arts approved the broadest restrictions ever on the content of NEA-funded art, banning not only works that are found to "depict . . . in a patently offensive way, sexual or excretory activities" but also those works that "denigrate the objects or beliefs of the adherents of a particular religion." But we do think it would be a mistake to label this book as one of blasphemy. *Sweet Jesus* is a collection of poetry that is full of longing and spiritual questioning about the ultimate icon, even when it is tongue in cheek, even when the longing is peculiar.

After John Lennon uttered his now-infamous declaration, one Alabama disc jockey, in an uproar, set off a firestorm that led to massive nationwide burnings of Beatles albums. Eventually, Lennon, pacifist that he was, told the preacher who demanded a public apology that he was sorry. According to Geoffrey Giuliano's

*The Lost Beatles Interviews*, Lennon couldn't stand the thought of anybody hating him for something irrational.

So it is in Lennon's spirit that *Sweet Jesus* was compiled. And it is our hope that the book will be read in that same sweet spirit.

Nick Carbó was born in the Philippines and raised in Manila. He is the author of *Secret Asian Man* (Tia Chucha Press, 2000) and *El Grupo McDonald's* (Tia Chucha Press, 1995) and the editor of *Returning a Borrowed Tongue: An Anthology of Filipino and Filipino American Poetry* (Coffee House Press, 1996). Among his awards are fellowships in poetry from the National Endowment for the Arts and the New York Foundation of the Arts.

Denise Duhamel's books of poetry include *Queen for a Day: Selected and New Poems* (University of Pittsburgh Press, 2001), *The Star-Spangled Banner* (Southern Illinois University Press, 1999) and *Kinky* (Orchises Press, 1997). Her work has been anthologized in four volumes of *The Best American Poetry* (2000, 1998, 1994 and 1993). She teaches poetry at Florida International University in Miami.

# STRANGE FAITH

SWEET JESUS

# Signs & Miracles

"If You exist," I said. "Send me
a pony."

Immediately Jesus appeared
in my bedroom.

I got off my knees. "You heard
my prayer!"

He quoted Himself: "Except ye
see signs and miracles, you will
not believe."

"Be reasonable, Jesus. It's hard
to just take Your word for it."

"But I'm here. In your bedroom.
Isn't that enough?"

"So is the pony outside?"

# Christmas Card

Outside the locker room this morning I heard
some guy say into the phone, "But, Jesus, I'd do
anything for you."

I suspect he wasn't talking to The Source,
more likely to a woman in El Sereno taking off
her uniform and name tag and staring at the tree.

Now the carols over the loudspeaker make me
wonder if Jesus is looking down at my Speedos
no bigger than a crucifixion panty.

I'm surprised You aren't fed up to here with us.
After all, what do we say except, "I want a pony!"
Never, "Thanks for my pretty feet and the salad tongs."

Well, here's a little something for Your birthday.
This last lap—as hard and as fast as I can—
is for You.

# The Feet Man

*—for Leo Dangel*

The worst job I ever had was nailing
Jesus' feet to the cross on the
assembly line at the crucifix factory.
Jesus! I'd never thought of myself
as religious before that, but when
I had to strike those nails—I figured
it up once—more than two thousand times
a day, my mind began seeing things:
little tremors along the skin, jerks of
those legs that were bonier than
model's legs, his eyes imploring,
forgiving. I swear, if a tiny drop of blood
had oozed out of that wood at my pounding,
I wouldn't have been surprised at all.
I was ripe for a miracle, or a vacation.
All I got was worse: with each blow
of the hammer, I flinched, as if I
were the one getting pierced. Doing
that job day after day was bad enough,
but doing it to myself—my arms

spread out from one end of my paycheck

to the other—was crazy. I began

to sweat constantly, though the place

was air-conditioned. It wasn't long before

the foreman took me aside and told me

I was taking my job too seriously, that

if I wanted to keep it I had better calm down.

He was right. I pulled myself together

like a man and put all pointless thoughts

out of my head. Or tried to. It wasn't easy:

imagine Jesus after Jesus coming down

at you along that line, and you with

your hammer poised, you knowing

what you have to do to make a living.

# At the Smithville Methodist Church

It was supposed to be Arts & Crafts for a week,
but when she came home
with the "Jesus Saves" button, we knew what art
was up, what ancient craft.

She liked her little friends. She liked the songs
they sang when they weren't
twisting and folding paper into dolls.
What could be so bad?

Jesus had been a good man, and putting faith
in good men was what
we had to do to stay this side of cynicism,
that other sadness.

O.K., we said. One week. But when she came home
singing "Jesus loves me,
the Bible tells me so," it was time to talk.
Could we say Jesus

doesn't love you? Could I tell her the Bible
is a great book certain people use

to make you feel bad? We sent her back
without a word.

It had been so long since we believed, so long
since we needed Jesus
as our nemesis and friend, that we thought he was
sufficiently dead,

that our children would think of him like Lincoln
or Thomas Jefferson.
Soon it became clear to us: you can't teach disbelief
to a child,

only wonderful stories, and we hadn't a story
nearly as good.
On parents' night there were the Arts & Crafts
all spread out

like appetizers. Then we took our seats
in the church
and the children sang a song about the Ark,
and Hallelujah

and one in which they had to jump up and down
for Jesus.
I can't remember ever feeling so uncertain
about what's comic, what's serious.

Evolution is magical but devoid of heroes.
You can't say to your child
"Evolution loves you." The story stinks
of extinction and nothing

exciting happens for centuries. I didn't have
a wonderful story for my child
and she was beaming. All the way home in the car
she sang the songs,

occasionally standing up for Jesus.
There was nothing to do
but drive, ride it out, sing along
in silence.

# The Son of Man

Late last night on State Street
I saw Jesus—or at least
a good facsimile—hustling.
He had it all:
the hair, the beard,
the piercing eyes,
the hot glare of a man
with hidden wounds.
But his righteous anger
sabotaged his efforts;
no one slowed their car
to wave him over;
no one loitered at the corner,
looking back.

This was not the gentle Jesus
of the sixties,
borne aloft by soft black voices.
This was the Jesus
turned out on the street
by Republican congressmen

who call their cruelty "reform."
This was the new orphan Jesus—
disowned, or just abandoned,
by his father.
This, too, was Jesus
on a burning cross, but no
Beatitudes would guide him.
This Jesus
did not have a dream.

I tried to scan him
but not catch his eye;
I was compelled,
but not at all attracted.
His hands, shoved in the pockets
of his grimy low-slung jeans,
could not be checked
for glowing wounds.
His sandaled feet
looked like they would pollute
most any water

they might walk on.
His chest was bare;
his side was bruised,
but whole.
He was fascinating
as a three-car crash
jamming the world's most mundane freeway.
He was the dark spot
in this sea of detail,
leaning on a brownstone wall.

When he caught me,
I was quick
to look away,
to walk away,
to get away;
he followed,
but just for a block.

I prayed my thanks
under my rapid breath;

his childhood and mine
would collide
like the nail and the wood.

All I could do
was save
myself.

# Jesus & Puberty

I was the same age as Jesus when he left home and taught in the temple. I sat on the edge of my life—the holy ghost was in my mouth, waters rose and fell around me— and I stepped like an eagle from her nest to begin. I knew everything that had come before, everything that would come after, I guess you could say I was obsessed with the hand gestures little Christ was making in the bible pictures, the way the learned men leaned their heads toward him, the possibilities of all that blood.

My blood descends like a million possible infants. On Halloween we have a party, boy-girl, then down my legs and into my socks, dark jelly, old cherry wine, my childhood slides into earth. Oh God, I say, for the first time meaning damn.

I could grow lighter now but you don't see me in the dark even with these pointy lights pointing blue and cool as raspberry ice. I'm digging deep into loam, forcing myself, a bulb in the thick of earth, everything in me begging to swell and burst. Where will I get the cash to feed my roots, where will my roots go when they've drunk all there possibly is to drink?

Jesus-Jesus-Bo-Jesus-Banana-Fana-Fo-Fesus-Fe-Fi-Mo-Mesus. He came to me in his Bo-Besus outfit, soiled but shiny raiment indicative of resurrection, the large sandals made in town by a leather smith. He said my name too softly as always and I was hooked.

Once he took me to the woods behind the brown split-level behind the old stone wall rife with rattlers and placed me on a rock. The rock was cold in summer, cold in winter, it sat below me and drew in my warmth. I was a small iron on its roof and it listened. Jesus flew among trees I named and gave persona to—twin elms, tall virgins. Everywhere figures of light came down from the Sun, and the child turned the rock warm, the rock blazed bright where the woman-child lay naming trees.

# On Getting Happy

She was like lots of women who find Jesus
on Sunday & leave him to his own devices
Monday. She was a skinny thing, all knees,
Hallelujah & Holy Ghostin'. Kristen dated a cat
no one much liked, got whapped upside the head
every now & again. No one reported this
to anyone who could make a difference.

Every Sunday, if the congregation was big
enough & our choir loud enough, Kristen's
glasses sprouted wings, her arms became
propellers, her legs: jackhammers. We ducked,
tucked & prayed. The Spirit, I was told,
is bigger than our bodies, hence her mad jerk.
I questioned Jesus that year & got no answer.

If getting happy is to be filled with Spirit,
if Sunday is just a word & we are siblings
of a single father, if we ignored Kristen's
cries, what were we filled with, what are we
filled with & does He care for our apologies
these many years later?

# Jesus Rum

All our growing up Jesus lived in our house
like one of those life-size, headless,
cardboard figures impoverished Victorians
posed behind, borrowing impossible finery
for photographs. We called His name
Father for it was your face and clerical collar
atop His neck, your tongue gutting us
with scorn and disgust and twisted logic
for that which you were about to do:
break our bodies in remembrance of Him.

We worshiped You, four little towheads,
all in a row, all bent double, hands on knees,
receiving the daily blessing of your belt
to help us, which You promised was serving us
right, which You promised we'd asked for, which
You promised hurt You more, our bare buttocks
turning red as blood around white welts, because
you promised, You were good, so almighty
good You even claimed your pain: You suffered
that we might not, and we loved You

as we could not love ourselves, with a love
that passeth all understanding, understanding
You knew not what You did, thereby
forgiving You, thereby protecting You
from finding out, afraid You'd die
if You knew You were not doing good,
if You knew You broke our insides
when You were drunk on Jesus, afraid we
would die if you stopped: what being had we,
that's mentionable, if we weren't "forgiving"

always unasked; what being had you if you asked?
I'd even forgiven you for stealing the face
of God from me, on top of any inner resource;
there were always newer lashings to forgive,
thank god; it was the only power I had, that and
never telling; the alternative was
separation, death as we are for both of us.
Whose arms were strong enough to hold you up
if we took away the skirts of Jesus? Whose head,
what heart, what arms for us if we gave up You?

But again you steal my child for Jesus,
this time the metaphor made flesh, the child
of my womb, of my heart, a child I could love,
waiting until she was luscious with my sweat
and sleepless nights, ripe with rebellion
for the plucking, filled with damnation
for not giving her this, for not giving her that,
scared of uncoupling. You began unbuckling,
saying, *Fear not,*

*for I am with you; My rod and My staff,*
*My wallet and My pity, shall comfort her, for I am*
*buying her all that she wants; I am feeding*
*Her righteousness for your own good;*
*this hurts Me more than you but you*
*asked for it; you will not listen; you will not*
*do as I say; if you wish to speak to her again*
*you will speak My language, for I am creating her*
*in My own image to serve you right,*
*for not going to church, for turning*
*to heathens when you had God, or Me;*

*I am restoring her soul; I am leading her into*
*My pastures, for the Fifth Commandment really means*
*only parents worthy of being honored shall be honored;*
*she shall not want for anything; I'll teach you*
*a lesson you'll never forget; I'll get you*
*back into the fold; I'll show you what for!*


My collapse, I am told, just goes to prove
I'm a poor loser. And no Christian. Or else
I'd get back on my feet and come with her, cleave
unto the father, unto the daughter, forever,
prop both of them up. Yea, his belt and coiled logic
have followed me all the days of my life until
he's hit me so hard he's knocked off
his head; all the holier-than-Thou-
and-him, hot-air nobility, all
the excusing, that which was
the body of us,
whiffs out the top of my neck.

I am a recovering Jesus,
dead to the old ways, living under a new law
unbuckling, recoiling, drying out
from my father, from my daughter possessed.

# Cranky Jesus

Yes, he was patient, and gentle, and good,
but one could argue that he'd not been truly tested.
Because you have to admit his life must have been cushy
what with the sinful and sickly too eager to worm
their way into his graces. And then yes,
those three terrible days, but they were only
days—they did not equal, say, a lifetime spent sheathed
waist-downward in supp-hose for the graveyard shift
at the Pancake Palace by the interstate. Where
in the stoppage of time between the drunks' nodding out
over pigs in a blanket and their rising near dawn
with a glaze of syrup on their faces, the night
parades its endless wants. For the steak more rare
and the eggs more runny, for Tabasco,
baking soda, jumper cables, nitroglycerine tabs.
At Calvary, they may have asked for his name
but not that it be worn in plastic Dymo lettering
stuck under, "Hello!" in the nametag blank;
suffering, yes, but not being forced to act chirpy,
not hearing *what'sa matter afraid a smile*
*might break your your face* every time he bends over

to palm the sixty cents in dimes and nickles
that is exactly fifteen percent of $3.99
plus an extra fraction of a penny that allows the world
to believe itself generous, the world pinking up now,
spinning the night's dregs into yet one more day
that he enters by running the gantlet of dumpsters,
him being a woman who curses the sun, the tweeting birds,
a woman whose body just rests, any kind of rest.

# Chubby Jesus

Imagine he'd swallowed whole pitchers of sweet cream,
wolfed down the cheese and the larded crust,
eaten rashers of bacon, the grease undercoating
the crumb-beard on his chin. Then see how it is

when the mind's reworkings leaven him like dough.
How everything changes when we nail him up
with a stomach that the wind set rippling, and thighs
at last of human girth, his pectoral muscles
like wax beads dripping from a flame. Oh, he is still

the son of man, but also the great white shark
at the maritime museum, suspended high
on such alarmingly slender threads that no one
dares to venture underneath. And if the lesson

we're to construe from his dying is about the body
being no more than a scarf wrapped around the inner life,
a length of chiffon flip—and flagging the trail
as the soul gets whisked off in a convertible
to the afterlife's Daytona Beach . . . well, why then

does the thumb have to run so often around the leghole
to liberate the elastic from the crack, why
does Aunt Ivy's heart give out there on the table
when some essential molecule of her gets liposucted out:

see: we *are* our lipo. And if there's a life after this one
in the too-rubbery human suit, let it take place north
of Vladivostock, somewhere we'll be able to resurrect
the armor of our early-70's junior high fake wolf fur-trimmed
snorkel coats. The soul will be out there

mewling on the trap line, though in this case
the hardware's post-Soviet low-tech, an apple carton
propped up on a stick. And no way to see inside
except by flipping up the box, whereupon

the animal is history: a thump, a blur, a gone.

# Lazy Jesus

Maybe it started as an excuse for idling
when Jesus got tired of banging on all that wood.
After years with the mallet, years with the adz,
his vertebrae nested like jagged stones.
Why not lie by the river with a couple of buddies,
passing a jug and naming each cloud's shape?
*Let's go down to the temple and upend some tables,*
one offers. *Let's pig out on fishfry*
*and wine.* Days they feel energetic
they'll roast a goat, its legs twirling
up then down then up then down until someone says *Hey*
*someone else take a turn spinning this damn stick.*

Could it be just coincidence he finally shows up
with Lazarus dead and the bedpan put away?
And notice how even the feast never ending
leaves him with not one dirty dish. You never see Jesus
wielding the sledge to the goat's blunt head—
though I could see in that office, yes:
he would know the kindest way to do the cruelest thing.
But not cleaning the moldy seal of the fridge

or batting the wasp nest from the eaves.
And he'll never show up at your door with a U-haul.
Not that he's the type of guy you'd want anyway
on the bottom of your sofa, going up a flight of stairs.

# Emptying Town

*—after Provincetown*

Each fall this town empties, leaving me
drained, standing on the dock, waving *bye-
bye,* the white handkerchief
stuck in my throat. You know the way Jesus

rips open his shirt
to show us his heart, all flaming & thorny,
the way he points to it. I'm afraid
the way I miss you

will be this obvious. I have

a friend who everyone warns me
is dangerous, he hides
bloody images of Jesus around my house

for me to find when I come home—Jesus
behind the cupboard door, Jesus tucked

into the mirror. He wants to save me
but we disagree from what. My version of hell
is someone ripping open his
shirt & saying,

*look what I did for you.*

# The Face of Jesús in Campbell's ABC Tomato Soup

*—for Johnny Cash*

While our daily soup simmers on the stove,
my grandmother claims Jesús's face has appeared
there out of the boiling liquid, a spattering shape
on the nicked porcelain stove, crown of thorns
and all. And last week it was La Caridad
in a burnt piece of toast.

        And the days pile up into each other: work,
school, the clothes we will send home or take to church
for the poor, or the resoled shoes my father leaves
like dead crows by the front door, or our three-legged
cat who dangles from the end of the patio's brick fence,
a mangled mockingbird in its bloody paws.

In my bowl of Campbell's tomato alphabet soup,
the word "surrender" blurps to life in the edges.
A mop next to an empty trough, a wood dove stopped
for a drink, but the trough is dried up, rusted through,
crabgrass grown in a tuft. If I say "Jesús," my mother
will think of blasphemy. My father is at work at this

hour. In his final hour he will clutch his heart
with both hands and say: "Cristo mio!" But nothing,
not even the blue-zap of electricity passing between
the paddles of a defibrillator can bring him back. Look
into my bowl and you will see my own reflection, a boy
of twelve—already lost in this foreign country, hands

held in prayer to this Christ of soup, and crimson words.

# His Body Like Christ Passed in and out of My Life

A woman selling Bibles at the Greyhound station.
Me waiting. I was not indifferent, only hardened.
A German violin instead of her voice. Headphones
in my ears. The smell of that place, diesel and Brahms.
Me waiting as others wait. Me turning the cassette,
she turning pages in that purgatory without deliverance.
Later my lover smiling as Jesus, always late, never
his fault. Me looking back at a woman praising God.
Her devotion. My envy. A desire for permanence.
For a world without betrayal. I think of that winter,
the tracks outside my window erased from a field
of snow, me ironing sheets as if no one had slept
there. A bus heading South without me. My car
not starting, dead batteries, an empty walkman
discarded under the bed. How the world slides away.
Me diminished by the thought of him. Of Spring.
What are birds returning, singing, compared to this,
the lives that I have forsaken to honor a god.

# Eucharist

*—for Diane*

1.

We are taught to take the bread
into our bodies
as proof of Jesus's body.

The bread is metaphor.
The bread is Jesus transubstantiated.
The bread is simply bread.

I have believed all three of those tenets
and taken each into my body
though I am Spokane Indian

and also take salmon
into my body
as proof of salmon.

The salmon is my faith returned.
The salmon is simply salmon.
The salmon is not bread.

2.
Suddenly, we are wed
and I am just as surprised as you
that marriage has become our bread.

You, the Hidatsa Indian
from the plains of North Dakota
who does not believe in salmon

and me, the Spokane, who
never trusted the hands of the priest
as he delivered the bread.

During Eucharist, I am afraid
to close my eyes. I want to see
what has been set on the table before me.

Look, this could be our first or last supper.
I don't know which meal would help me believe
that we have become sacred.

Sweetheart, are we the stone
rolled from the mouth
of the tomb that could not keep him?

Sweetheart, are we the salmon
rising from the waters
that have been their home for centuries?

Sweetheart, are we baptism?
Are we the flesh and blood?
Are we the washing of feet?

3.
If that was Easter
then the church was full
as we stood against the wall

praying for an empty pew.
If that was Easter
then I rose that morning

in love with you
though I rise every morning
more or less

in love with you.
If that was Easter
then you were asked

to be the Eucharistic minister
and replace the woman
who said she wanted to sing

in the choir instead.
If that was Easter
then you held the bread

to my mouth
and I swallowed it whole.
Amen, amen. Amen.

# Simple

When the wafer dissolves on my tongue I won-
der what part of the Lord I have eaten,
His scrotum molecularly recon-
structed in a pale disc, or a wheaten
flap of armpit? Perhaps internal organs
vaporized to universal atoms
from the thorax of our Lord. Others had plans
to preserve the saints in bits, the phantom
of Anthony's larynx in a ruby vase,
Agatha's breasts in gold caskets, the flesh
reserved. I only eat our Lord and mas-
ticate the host, the church a crèche,
and I in my stall not even knowing how
to blow glass housing for a saint or wield
a hammer with my hoof, unable to bow
or scoop breasts into a box. The world
transubstantiates me to animal
evolving in reverse: soon I could be a lizard
on the wall of the manger, in time one-celled,
perhaps a single cell of the baby Lord,
perhaps His tongue, so what I chew as symbol
I might at last become: simple.

# Purple Jesus

Jesus, I'm not done with You.
Are You done with me?
Last week I stopped in a church
to look at a box they say
holds some holy bones
just to say I was there.

You have to take it on faith
that I was there, that I saw the box,
that the bones were in the box,
that the bones were St. Valentine's,
that St. Valentine was a holy man,
holy enough to join the frat,
that the people who let him in
weren't fools to begin with,
filling each other's underwear
with shaving cream.
You see what I'm saying?
I haven't even got anywhere near
what it takes to believe in You.

*

I walked in to the smell
of Purple Jesus
rising in sweet incense
like one beautiful letter
repeating itself above our heads.
Purple Jesus makes me shut up
and admire the dust I'm headed for.

My mother can't kneel anymore.
She sits during the kneeling parts—
on the edge of the pew so she's not quite
comfortable, so her knees almost
touch the kneeler. She believes
the somber Purple Jesus knows
she'd be kneeling
if it didn't hurt
quite so much.

*

Purple Jesus, my favorite crayon.
You don't make me a soldier
in Your army. You don't ask for
the numb repeated prayer.
You simply want my sadness.

I go in churches as a tourist
to look at art made in Your name.
One Good Friday I stood in back
with my arms crossed, and an angry
man made me unfold them.
If that's all it takes
to dis You,
I'm in trouble.

\*

We don't get to see the Purple Jesus
very often, though when I smoked
a lot of pot, I imagined I saw Him often.

I meant no disrespect.
I mean no disrespect.
Lord have Mercy.
Christ have Mercy.

If I was going to rise from the dead,
spring would be the time.
I am writing a name in the layered sunset.
Mine, not His.

# The Boogie-Down Dancers

*(Triptych—three studies for a crucifixion, 1962)*

The Man in the Middle—
how can we picture Him without
long hair and a beard, the one old hippie
who still goes to all the concerts,
gray streaks in His hair, jeans still hip-
hugging. Shirtless whenever possible.

At any single moment
at least 43 Jesuses exist
in the world. Kinda
franchisey.

No i.d. cards.
Faith is a liability
you can't get insurance for.
Stop me before I get too pithy.

\*

Creating facts,
His greatest gift.

There were no thieves
on either side of Him—
those were the boogie-down
dancers shakin' their thangs.

At what point
did their bodies give in,
drop to the dust?
What music played
in their heads,

the three of them
doing leaps and spins, splits,
Pilate tapping his shoes?

# Christ at the Apollo, 1962

*—for Andrew Hudgins*

*Even in religious fervor there is
a touch of animal heat.*
—Walt Whitman

Despite the grisly wounds portrayed in prints,

the ropy prongs of blood stapling His eyes

or holes like burnt half-dollars in His feet,

the purple gash a coked teenybopper's

lipsticked mouth in His side, Christ's suffering

seemed less divine than the doubling-over

pain possessing "the hardest working man."

I still don't know whose wounds were worse: Christ's brow

thumb-tacked with thorns, humped crowns of feet spike-split—

or James Brown's shattered knees. It's blasphemy

to equate such ravers in their lonesome

afflictions, but when James collapsed on stage

and whispered *please please please,* I rocked with cold,

forsaken Jesus in Gethsemane

and, for the first time, grasped His agony.

Both rose, Christ in His unbleached muslin gown

to assume His rightful, heavenly throne,

James wrapped in his cape, pussy-pink satin,

to ecstatic whoops of his fans in Harlem.

When resurrection tugs, I'd rather let

the Famous Flames clasp my hand to guide me

than proud Mary or angelic orders

still befuddled by unbridled passion.

Pale sisters foistered relics upon me,

charred splinter from that chatty thief's cross and

snipped thread from the shroud that xeroxed Christ's corpse,

so I can't help but fashion the future—

soul-struck pilgrims prostrate at the altar

that preserves our Godfather's three-inch heels

or, under glass, like St. Catherine's skull, *please*,

his wicked, marceled conk, his tortured knees.

# Jesus is Just Alright

SWEET JESUS

# Goodtime Jesus

Jesus got up one day a little later than usual. He had been dreaming so deep there was nothing left in his head. What was it? A nightmare, dead bodies walking all around him, eyes rolled back, skin falling off. But he wasn't afraid of that. It was a beautiful day. How 'bout some coffee? Don't mind if I do. Take a little ride on my donkey, I love that donkey. Hell, I love everybody.

# The Jesus Infection

Jesus is with me

on the Blue Grass Parkway going eastbound.

He is with me

on the old Harrodsburg Road coming home.

I am listening

to country gospel music

in the borrowed Subaru.

The gas pedal

and the words

leap to the music.

O throw out the lifeline!

Someone is drifting away.

Flags fly up in my mind

without my knowing

where they've been lying furled

and I am happy

living the sunlight

where Jesus is near.

A man is driving his polled Herefords

across the gleanings of a cornfield

while I am bound for the kingdom of the free.
At the little trestle bridge that has no railing
I see that I won't have to cross Jordan alone.

Signposts every mile exhort me
to Get Right With God
and I move over.
There's a neon message blazing
at the crossroad
catty-corner to the Burger Queen:
Ye Come With Me.
It is well with my soul, Jesus?
It sounds so easy
to be happy after sunrise,
to be washed in the crimson flood.

Now I am tailgating
and I read a bumper sticker
on a Ford truck full of Poland Chinas.
It says: Honk If You Know Jesus
and I do it.

My sound blasts out for miles
behind the pigsqueal
and it's catching in the front end,
in the axle,
in the universal joint,
this rich contagion.

We are going down the valley on a hairpin turn,
the swine and me, we're breakneck in
we're leaning on
the everlasting arms.

# Jesus Saves

This dude *Jesus Saves*
must be popular or something:
You see his name everywhere.
I first saw it when I woke up
from a Bunker Hill cardboard box
to a huge sign near the top
of the L.A. library.
It read: *"Jesús Saves."*

I wish I were that guy . . .
then I wouldn't be
this chocked-faced pirate on city
seas, this starved acrobat of the alcoves
loitering against splintered doors.
Then I wouldn't be this aberration
who once had a home, made of stone even,
and a woman to call wife.
In the old country,
I worked since I was seven!
I knew the meaning
of the sun's behest

for pores to weep.
But now such toil is allowed
to rot like too many berries on a bush.

In the old country, I laughed the loudest,
made the most incisive remarks
and held at bay even the most
limpid of gatherings.

But here I am a grieving poet,
a scavenger of useless literature;
they mean nothing in this place . . .
my metaphoric manner,
the spectacle of my viscous verse
—nothing!
I am but a shadow on the sidewalk,
a spot of soot on a block wall;
a roll of dice tossed across
a collapsing hallway in a downtown
SRO hotel.

Ok, *Señor Saves,* right now this is your time.
But someday a billboard
will proclaim my existence.
Someday people will sigh my name
as if it were confection on the lips.
As long as I have a rhythm in my breast,
there will come this fine day
when this orphan, pregnant with genius,
is discovered sprouting epiphanies like wings
on the doorstep of
mother civilization.

# Uncle

At nine I knew what Jesus would do
if he got C.O. just for being born
Mennonite. He'd go away, like you.

In the name of peace, he'd race
an ambulance through the screaming streets
of Saigon. He'd grow a moustache to show
he wasn't a soldier—a speck
on the camera lens, Grandpa insisted.

He'd take a generator to a village
in the hills where golden children
would run behind him yelling, "Mother Fucker."

He'd thrust brilliant green blades
of rice into the fields where men's legs
and torsos of water buffaloes exploded
when plows struck bombs in the mud.

When the planes returned, he'd load
whomever he could into the only car,

drive to a refugee camp, and there give up
at last, as you gave up bearing the war
on your tall, blond body.

Lost across the continents for months,
you returned to us, the uncle of someone else,
gaunt as a corpse, pale and haunted.
And when you could barely finish
a child's portion at Howard Johnson's,
that was the only miracle I could grasp.

# Just Spring

The teenage boys who broke into
Our Lady of the Sacred Heart
to graffiti their new vocabulary
of swear words on the white white walls
were attracted enough by the church, at least,
to vandalize it.

They broke the virgin's plaster nose
with baseball bats
and marked her private parts with orange spray paint
because they loved their mothers so much
it was killing them

but they left the gaunt, adolescent torso of Jesus
hanging on the wall, untouched,
because they didn't recognize themselves.

Or maybe it's just Spring,
which drives more than birds and flowers crazy.

Desire, someone says,

polishing his turbo-charged Camaro in the drive,

running his hand over its curves,

it's a bitch.

The blurred blue letters of the name Dianne

scorched into his forearm

record a season in his life

he probably regrets,

but desire, if you don't let it out, everybody knows

backs up and poisons you inside

like old sap clogged inside a tree

or like the hard line of JoAnn's mouth

when she said,

speaking of her first and recently demolished marriage,

Never Again,

gripping the steering wheel

and jamming the gas pedal

down into the floor

though she probably still wants
to be followed, pulled over,
taken from her car and carried off
into the heavenly tall grass
of heterosexual imagination,

and kissed all over her thirty-nine-year-old body
until, like Spring,
she comes and comes and comes.
Suffering Mother of God. Sweet Jesus.

# Jesus, the Perfect Lover

2000 years and he's still rising.
I know, I know, girls. If Hell didn't exist before,
it does now. Just for my mouth. But if I explained

how his skin feels, how timeless and damp,
how raw and in need of bandaging
from my constant, constantly

forgiven touch,
you'd toss your hair one last time
and put on your suit of flames too.

How often have we all said, "If only
I never had to leave the house again, if only
my wishes were fishes and my supernatural boyfriend

could make thousands more of them, if only no one else
ever existed at all." My Jesus spreads himself out
permanently and looks a lot like me:

a bit disappointed but not too surprised. Still, he's glad

that he can at least distract me from whatever

crude nails my palms have room for.


But look how he hangs so quietly—there's definitely

an ingredient missing. Someone very large

didn't think it through and forgot


to add absolute strength.

So he's my undressed apology,

my portable laboratory


where "Dear Lord, no" and My God, yes"

were simultaneously invented.

I can tell by the amused look in his eye


that, straddling and blond

and incomplete, I am not responsible

for what I do. Mostly, though, the way

we squirm together

is like sleep, only brighter.

After I press against him


for an hour or two, he can see right through me.

He knows the glint of my ribs,

the steam escaping my heart.


Any fool can see

how he looks down at me,

wanting to hold me, extinguish me, wishing


he would've thought of this before,

of everything he could have done for me

with his arms. That's what makes him perfect,


he always admits

to my burning image

when he's wrong.

# Night Light

in pure white
plastic
the lord Jesus Christ
as a man
carrying a small plastic lamb
is plugged
into the bathroom socket

he's six inches tall and erect
hanging on the wall
over the toilet
lighting the way
for me
from the bedroom
in the middle of the night

and every month
on the second day
of my menses
when I can't get through
the night
without changing my pad
Jesus is there
for me

# Gold Jesus

*—after Jim Daniels*

Someone poured the sun
into your iron cast, let you cool.
Someone polished your wounds

until we saw our faces.
Last night your voice came to me
disguised as a high note

Miles Davis blew out of his trumpet,
pure as the silence that followed.
Rumor has it you've got honey-blood,

a hive for a heart. That
and some of your bees are dying,
entire swarms unhooking from the sky.

There now. It's better than
most of us—fingernails silvered
from lottery tickets,

dollar signs buzzing
in our heads, a chunk of fool's gold
behind every left nipple.

# Ode to Money

While looking at the frescoes of the life of St. Peter
      in the Brancacci chapel in Florence,
I hear Megan say the theme of the series is money,
      and I think, you could probably say the same
about most of our lives, having it, getting it,
      spending it, hoarding it, lording it over others,
letting it slip through our fingers, and while most of us
      are not usurers like Felice Brancacci,
who had to commission a chapel to avoid going to hell,
      making ends meet is something that occupies
our minds from time to time, and if time is money,
      is all money eternally present,
or is it the fourth dimension:
      height, width, depth and money?
I'm no Einstein, but I'd say yes, or why are money
      and art thick as thieves,
and while Jesus said render unto Caesar
      that which is Caesar's and to God
that which is God's, sometimes it's not easy
      to figure out which is which, or who is who,
as when Pope Pius made his deal with Hitler,

or when tax time rolls around, who's god there,
you or the IRS? Because in the Brancacci Chapel,
        when Jesus sends St. Peter out to fetch
a piece of gold from a fish's mouth, I must say
        the fish looks as surprised as anyone,
he's ejecting coins like a slot machine in Reno.
        Most of us have to toil in pretty stony soil
to earn our daily bread, filling out forms,
        counting money, sitting in meetings
so boring our brains turn to liquid
        and drip out our ears, writing gorgeous
sentences for those who would not recognize
        beauty if it announced itself
in full Louis XIV Sun King regalia
        and handed out party favors.
Half the time I'm counting my cash
        like Jacob Marley in hell
and the other half throwing it out the windows
        of Cadillac convertibles while I cruise
through Memphis with Elvis. Oh, simoleons, spondulicks,
        shekels, mazuma, what I wouldn't give for a grand,

a C-note, a sawbuck, two bits, an IOU from anyone,

       even Zelda Fitzgerald, who would probably not

be whispering "Waste not, want not," or "A penny saved

       is a penny earned" into my pearly ear.

In Rome looking at Caravaggio's The Calling

       of St. Matthew, there's the money theme again

because Matthew and his repulsive cronies

       are counting coins on a table as Jesus

holds out his hand to beckon the tax collector

       into his doomed if divine fold,

and you've got to wonder what enticement

       he could be offering such a one

as Matthew, because let's face it

       he would not be saying to anybody, anyway,

any time, you gotta have money, honey,

       if you wanna dance with me.

# Poem in Which Christ Is Spotted on the Bowery, NYC

Vinny Borriello and I argued cool those grade school afternoons,
whole lunch hour debates in the church yard: Fonzie, Captain Kirk,
Evel Knieval; our heroes. When Sister Gertrude rang the brass bell that yelled for us
to stop running and summoned us to alignment,
we always strayed to the right or left. In St. Charles Church
on Lenten Fridays we walked the Stations of the Cross, Christ's pain
plainly displayed: a role model for some seventh graders

saving money in at-home mission boxes, but not
for us. The sun licked the stained glass brilliant like trilling stage lights
in clubs, years later. The stations of the subways our new religion; Sunday
sabbath at CBGB beside the men's shelter where Bleecker Street ended.
Maybe Christ walked the Bowery
in 1983. On TV the Moral Majority begged for Franklins
and news shows broadcast stories of punk rock

violence to keep our mothers awake and praying late along the glass decades
of ten dollar rosaries. Vinny wore a black rosary
around his neck. I abdicated
my desk at St. Peter's Academy while my favorite band played
"Praise the Lord and Pass the Ammunition." At rallies

Nicaraguan men sang the Lord's Prayer in the Spanish
of coffee bean fields like nothing
I learned from Brother Cormack. They wanted a Prince of Peace to broker a treaty

allowing cousins to shake hands across the long expanse of ideology
and between the pews of mission churches. Vinny painted
Christ in an electric chair
on his black leather jacket, declared if the Messiah arrived then
they'd execute him. Or excommunicate him, I joked although truly I believed
he wouldn't have been sentenced to death
nor to a prison's labyrinth of tile floors and fluorescent lights
where tired-and-tough lifers would spend cigarettes for his hair. Nor
would he lay his nights on park benches or shelter mattresses.
No, I believe
he would've toured the country in a beat up Chrysler van,
with a four-piece band and a worn Fender Stratocaster
camouflaged with bumper stickers of his favorite groups.
J.C. and the Good News.

Their roadies:
the apostles. St. Peter running the fan club. I could even see

Sister Gertrude in one of their t-shirts. Imagine him
diving from the stage and walking the water of the crowd.
Five bucks a head. . . . Instead, all we had were Minor Threat, Reagan Youth, Heart
Attack. We had peace rallies in the rain and

tattoos in suburban basements from artists
known for their Christ heads or biker skulls. We slam danced through
Sunday afternoons for those three years we thought would stretch
a decade, but were just another adolescence, an attitude.
It all seems passé in an age
when stigmata might be body art. I recall sitting on a dumpster
watching police across the street break up
a posse of skinheads. And a preacher with leaflets
on the corner, was he praying for them or himself
when he muttered in that downpour?
If I knew where Vinny were I wouldn't call;

what do we have to say? Fact is: I knew people
who believed in nothing but rain. And newsprint
in the gutter. And the glitter of glass shards mixed
in the asphalt. I'm trying to explain

the way they caught the lowly glow of Lower East Side street lights

so they glimmered like nothing of the natural earth;

how from the right angle we could make out

a mosaic in the rain-slicked tarmac

as if some cathedral's great lead window had left its ghost

down there; so beautiful and random

that I might almost believe for a moment in a grace incarnate.

# Missing Bejesus

I lost something essential when the collision occurred. I lost it when the impact scared the bejesus out of me.

I was walking across several lanes of traffic when I felt the contact of a car against my person and the meeting of my body with the pavement. I was so scared I didn't have time to pray or curse, to shout *What the dickens!* or *What the deuce!*

Aside from the absence of my sweet bejesus, I was fine. I still had the living daylights. I could still dance with the devil. I just didn't have a personal relationship with the ineffable power anymore. I was staring into bloody hell, and I needed to rekindle my faith.

# "How Would Jesus Drive?"

*—painted on a truck, Ohio Turnpike*

Well, there would be no road rage, that's for sure.
Smoothly shifting down the entrance ramps,
never hogging the passing lane or driving
twenty miles with his left blinker on,
he would wave joyfully to kids in passing cars,
he would leave clear dry road behind
even in the worst sleet storm or blizzard.

In truth, he would be a bit of a pain in the butt,
lingering forever at intersections, letting others
go first, stopping motorists to alert them
to better driving techniques, announcing
to the big-rig drivers at the truck stop
that they should all abandon their loads
immediately, pile in his van for the long haul
to salvation—

       leaving those eighteen-wheelers
with emptied cabs in the parking lot,
rumbling as they spew diesel exhaust
into the sinful air, all their cargoes
of milk or oranges slowly going bad.

# Jesus Never Sleeps

Downstairs neighbors quicken
each morning before we wake—

Jesus-rock litany, gospel aerobics
rising through our mattress

like heat from winter's
sullen garden.

Their joyful noise banishes fat.
I see them toned

and electric as the guitars
they haul to weekend revival,

trim and unflappable
as game show hosts.

What blameless sport, to feel
the beat in your bones

and call it God! Here
to declare moral joy

in these corruptible bodies,
these latter days.

Our sleep, though—we cannot
love another's glee

rousting us from languid
heartfast dreams,

and blear as we curse
each tribal thump.

Yet who if not some antic god
unglues our eyes, opens

our mouths to sabbath naming,
and thrusts these two

nonbelievers into their own
bodies' good news?

# Kung Pao Christ

Driven across miles of deerpath highway to this link
our tastebuds remember as city and sizzle,
Szechuan and Hunan—even Thai and Indian buffets

on alternating weekends—we settle in a corner
across from the elderly couple who ask
if the Chinese New Year brings a new calendar,

new months, a fresh marking of the passage of time,
and the man's shaky fedora tips like he's seen
enough days to stop counting forward in any hurry.

This over-extended menu seems just right
on a late January night when smalltown cute,
"Kountry Cookin'" glacially surrounds us

like a slow-moving tomb of arteriosclerosis.
But it's only the graying winter slush—we hope that's all—
until a woman and a boy come in and sit across from us.

He's her grandson we find out over our hot and sour soup,
their conversation bridging the quiet space between us
in this otherwise empty restaurant all too easily,

and they act like any other generationally-challenged pair might
until after they've ordered the crispy duck and "King Pa" chicken,
and as we split the order of spring rolls, basting the shells

with mustard and fluorescent-orange sweet-and-sour sauce,
they begin their discussion of the Rapture,
or at least what sounds like a sermon on Last Days,

though the peculiar twists and tracks of these
new Revelations show an inspiration fitting
the end of the Millennium in a cathode-ray confessional.

The souls rising won't need bodies from the grave
but they'll get them anyway, their flesh like
Salvation Army toss-outs clinging like a net or

overcoat to cover something garbled
between the boy's admiring responses of *Cool*
to Grandma's calling ministrations. He says,

"They don't tell us nothing like this in Sunday school—
just boring Adam and Eve junk." If the woman hears him
it doesn't slow her down while she sinks us all

into the Bottomless Pit where in her tomorrow
we will perish if we stand with the goats and not the lambs,
where the Beast that is Satan rules, marked and ready

to sacrifice pigs against the tenets of Hebrew Law
before he turns to human sacrifice—one hundred
and forty-four thousand Jewish virgins . . .

We both hear her more clearly than the flavors
of the cloying impression of Moo Goo Gai Pan
can satisfy or the black bean sauce lost in Bell peppers

and red onions like a Southwestern mélange
of all the wrong tastes in all the wrong places.
As if a perverse angel programmed the five-years-

behind-the-times Adult Contemporary station
subbing for Muzak, a song slips through
the prophetic Babel around us: *Jesus he knows me,*

*and he knows I'm right. Been talking to Jesus*
*for all my life* . . . A Genesis hit—a band
that sold out artistically after its lead singer,

who was once a flower on stage in those heady
art-rock-psychedelic-silly days, left to become Peter Gabriel.
No, this Genesis owes all its glory to the commercial

smirk and swagger, the balding bravado of Phil Collins.
And if music can deliver us from evil,
from the impulse within to answer the darkness

that is not our own, not our business or belief,
this song saves us, gives us strength to turn our thoughts
away from the obvious, begging intrusion that devils us all.

So even when the crispy duck arrives golden
and spread forth like a cruciform icon the boy heartily tears
from its tender bed of wilting lettuce, when the waiter

tells the woman she made the best choice,
the spicy peanuts and meat the restaurant's most requested dish
—"watch out for the hot spicy peppers, please"—

even when her grandson says, "So was like Mary a virgin? . . .
That's awesome!," and she begins to explain how
Mary was "conceived by the Holy Spirit,"

we can look away, to each other, to the cookies
like delicate parcels and fortunes that read,
*You will make much out of a small thing*, and

*You do well adapting in a new environment,*
to the bill and the New Year's token wrapped in red
and gold paper, an unexpected gift, the latest discount.

# Dear Ann

I've been trying
to write you a letter.
I need help
in discerning my vocation
and in pulling together
the strands of my new reality.
When I accepted the notion
of carrying Jesus' yoke,
the homoerotic yearning
I'd been sitting on
emerged.
But Jesus is elusive.
He talks about finding
the narrow gate,
not taking
the wide, easy road,
and disappears into the crowd
to avoid his foes.
Yes, I connect Jesus
with being gay.
How to deal with it

is problematic.
Walls are coming down,
whether I push or not,
like mustard seed,
once it gets into your garden,
you can't get rid of it.

# Born Again

In the dream
I reach into my shirt,
grab my ribs,
tear my chest open.
Jesus emerges
saying,
"The spirit is
as a reversible robe."

One too-long book after another,
a daily bath of scripture,
a few semesters in seminary,
to figure out
who this Mediterranean peasant is
and why he has me by the balls.

And yes, Pat Robertson,
I'm saved!
Here I stand,
a 56-year-old virgin queer,
a repressed bourgeois
hiding a flaming queen.
Thank you, Jesus.

# Jesus Is Hanging over the Lesbian

A lesbian's mother and a preacher
are standing over the lesbian.

They are trying to cast out the demons.

Jesus is hanging over the lesbian,
but more concerned with his own demons,
head tilted back, dry blood remnants
of a demon's crown on his head.

The lesbian can not see Jesus.
The preacher is blocking her view
and she is waiting for her leg hairs
to grow like vines, wrap around the preacher's
head until he splits open, until she could see
what was really inside him.

The lesbian wonders how the demons got to her.
And as the concerned members of the community joined
in the casting out of the demons, Jesus slips down from the cross
without anyone noticing (they are all looking at the lesbian).

"Kind of like Baptism," he says, laughs.

"Jesus, I have had unnatural passions for women."

"Understandable," Jesus says, "they are very beautiful, don't let them fool you, even the grass has passions."

Jesus lifts himself back to the cross.

The lesbian's lover has a voice that sounds like Jesus
and persuades her to swim that night
in the river. The lesbian tosses her shirt,
and as her lover dips her head
back into the river, Jesus makes a sound
that echoes through the empty church,
a sound like a baby crying,
a sound like some blade of grass
had just been touched.

# Sons

We're Jewish, Father said.
So we don't believe in Christ.
If God wanted us to worship Jesus
he would have arranged for us to be born
into an Italian family. I have nothing
against Him. He was probably a very nice man.
You have to give Him credit for trying.
A lot of people still believe He's the Son of God.
I don't know what He had against His real father.
But if you ever did that to me,
said you were someone else's son, I'd be insulted.

# Apocryphal Jesus

# Prayer

Sweet Jesus, let her save you, let her take
your hands and hold them to her breasts,
slip the sandals from your feet, lay your body down
on sheets beaten clean against the fountain stones.
Let her rest her dark head on your chest,
let her tongue lift the fine hairs like a sword tip
parting the reeds, let her lips burnish
your neck, let your eyes be wet with pleasure.
Let her keep you from that other life, as a mother
keeps a child from the brick lip of a well,
though the rope and bucket shine and clang,
though the water's hidden silk and mystery call.
Let her patter soothe you and her passions
distract you; let her show you the light
storming the windows of her kitchen, peaches
in a wooden bowl, a small moon of gray cloth
she has sewn to her skirt to cover the tear.
What could be more holy than the curve of her back
as she sits, her hands opening a plum.
What could be more sacred than her eyes,
fierce and complicated as the truth. Your life

rising behind them. Your name on her lips.
Stay there, in her bare house, the black pots
hung from pegs, bread braided and glazed
on the table, a clay jug of violet wine.
There is the daily sacrament of rasp and chisel,
another chair to be made, shelves to be hewn
clean and even and carefully joined
to the sun-scrubbed walls, a small knife
for whittling abandoned scraps of wood
into toys and spoons for the children.
O Jesus, close your eyes and listen to it,
the air is alive with birdcalls and bees,
the dry rustle of palm leaves,
her distracted song as she washes her feet.
Let your death be quiet and ordinary.
Either life you choose will end in her arms.

# Divine Self-Determination

Halfway up the hill
Jesus has a change of heart,
makes a break for it.
The cross goes down
and he's off, the angry mob
right behind him, following
the trail of his stigmata.
The chase scene is long
and of course the Romans
join in, crashing chariots
into peddlers, each other.
But Jesus is fast
and winds his way
through back alleys
and then straight
into the heat of the desert.
The mob tries to bear down,
but they're mostly drunk
and as noted, Jesus is fast.
When capture looks hopeless.
they stagger as one, shrug
and say, Ah, let's forget
the whole thing. And we do.

# Descending Theology: The Crucifixion

To be crucified is first to lie down
on a shaved tree, and then to have oafs stretch you out
on a crossbar as if for flight, then thick spikes
      fix you into place.

Once the cross pops up and the pole stob
sinks vertically in an earth hole perhaps
at an awkward list, what then can you blame for hurt
      but your own self's burden?

You're not the figurehead on a ship. You're not
flying anywhere, and no one's coming to hug you.
You hang like that, a sack of flesh with the hard
      trinity of nails holding you into place.

Thus hung, your ribcage struggles up
to breathe until you suffocate, give up the ghost.
If God permits this, one wonders how
      this twirling earth

manages to navigate the gravities and star tugs.
Or if some less than loving watcher
watches us scuttle across the boneyard greens
        under which worms

seethe and the front jaws of beetles
eventually clasp toward the flesh of every beloved.
The man on the cross under massed thunderheads feels
        his soul leak away,

then surge. Some windy authority lures him higher
till an unseen tear in the sky's membrane is rent,
and he's streaming light, snatched back, drawn close,
        so all loneliness ends.

# Dead Christ

There seems no reason he should've died. His hands
are pierced by holes too tidy to have held,
untorn, hard muscles as they writhed on spikes.
And on the pink, scrubbed bottom of each foot
a bee-stung lip pouts daintily.
No reason he should die—and yet, and yet
Christ's eyes are swollen with it, his mouth
hangs slack with it, his belly taut with it,
his long hair lank with it, and damp;
and underneath the clinging funeral cloth
his manhood's huge and useless with it: Death.

One blood-drop trickles toward his wrist. Somehow
the grieving women missed it when they bathed,
today, the empty corpse. Most Christs return.
But this one's flesh. He isn't coming back.

# Monday Morning Always Brings Us

Jesus wakes from a carpenter's nap,
from a dream like a cartoon—
like he was a person only in mind,
he was an appropriated format:
was dead, even as his hair, nails
kept growing across glossless glooms,
then a cave, tunnel, a klieg light,
*on an empty stage, I snapped-to . . .*
*to find this funerary architecture true.*
*Deca-logy and defuncty, I only muse—*
*What the hell did I drink last night?*
He sees a thing in street clothes, wings
holding his Father's bubbling level—
*I've risen and I can't ever get down.*

# Ether Talk

Photo of Christ
on the fridge.

He and I, smoke.
All three of us

are humming.
A gust twitches

the kitchen window's
plastic wedge.

I see a neighbor
at tai chi, posing

like a Giacometti.
Two sides of a piece.

Every shape
is a way out.

From down the block
we hear teen tuneage:

Bad bad fucking very bad.
Autumn: winter exudes

the air. I boil water.
The thing to do.

Autumn: maker of ghost,
moon loser.

Jesus puffs.
I light one, too.

With all this
elongation

I don't wish
to appear rude.

# Christ As a Young Man

I've had my ear to the hive
for some time now, curious
for the buzz of many bodies
and thought of taking the papery house
home with me without anyone or any bee
seeing me. I even held it in my hand
once at the beginning of the summer;
it was still the size of a lemon and alive
with the labor of so many that
when I let it go with something less than gentleness

they flew out, who thought so many,
with honey and anger on their wings.

# The Cursing of the Fig Tree

*(Mark 11:12-23)*

While the apostles slept, or dully
gazed at the afternoon sky, desiring
some woman of Galilee,

or remembering the foam on a demon's mouth,
or wondering how the damned thing would end,
Christ leaned for a while on a fig tree

and found himself strangely hungry,
touching it leaf by leaf
as if parting the lips of the dumb.

# Teen Jesus

There are a few apocryphal stories about Jesus as a child:
how He walked up a sunbeam and flabbergasted His
playmates, how His bath water could cure any illness.

But there are no stories about Him as a teenager.
Did he make His bed without being told, or was He
the kind of boy who jumped out from behind bushes,
scaring girls on their way to the well, making
them drop those picturesque amphoras.

Did Mary nag Him about outgrowing His robes
and sandals: "Jesus, do You think Your father
and I are made out of myrrh?"

He was probably a cool kid, one the others looked up to.
It wasn't only that He said He wouldn't live very long.
A lot of the guys said that, especially the ones who
drank too much wine and raced their donkeys. Jesus
was different. While everybody else partied by the Dead
Sea, he'd take the rowboat out, step right off the bow,
and sink like a stone. Then he'd swim back in all mad.

His pals could tease Him out of a bad mood, though.
Pretty soon, He'd change water into beer and make one
hot dog feed everybody. Girls liked him, but He wasn't
into them, though no way was He like Obadiah, who made
his own curtains.

Nobody was surprised when He left home. A few
almost tagged along. But they couldn't resist Esther's
long hair pulled back and fastened with an amber pin,
or the pale underside of Miriam's wrist. So they got
married and never went more than five miles from
Nazareth.

When they heard about the crucifixion, their wives just
nodded. "I hate to say it, but I told you so."

# Jesus, Mary, and Joseph

Breakfast. Mary's had it with the whining—Just wait till your father gets home, young man—with the whining, the indolence, the back-talk and sass, the surliness. And don't even think you're going to sit around the house all summer, Mister. She taps a drop of Sucaryl into her coffee, lights up a Salem. I asked you nicely to turn off the TV. Now I'm telling you. One . . . two . . . If I have to get off this chair, you'll be one sorry little savior. Thank you. Sometimes she wishes she'd had a girl, someone she could shop with, gab with, someone to make dresses for, someone whose hair she could style—not some little prince who thinks the world should wait on him hand and foot. Go to your room if you're going to pout. Go! And close the door. I don't need to listen to you wasting your time.

Lunch. Mary gives Jesus a ten, tells him to run down to Ace of Subs for take-out. Get me a medium meatball with provolone. And a large RC. Get whatever you want for yourself. She tells him to grab the leash and take Satan. He needs the exercise. Jesus rolls his eyes. She says, You wanted the goddamned dog, but I'm the one who feeds him, bathes him, cleans up after him. You're going to walk him! Mary flops on the couch. She thinks, How could this have happened? You marry an older man for security, not for love. And then you find out that security is a kind of death. She looks around the apartment, at the white walls and the plaid furniture. She shakes her head. Security? she thinks. I married a carpenter. What kind of guy grows up in the desert, looks around at the sand, the rocks, the treeless waste, and says, I want to work with wood?

Supper. Joseph tries to explain why he's a little short with the paycheck this week. Needed a new bandsaw. Mary says, You think you had a bad day? You want to hear about my day with your son? No, Joseph says, he doesn't. I want a brewski. I want supper. I want the six o'clock news. The last thing I want is a headache. Mary tells him to put a shirt on before he comes to the table. Why? Because we're civilized, that's why. Joe, you need to talk to the boy. I'm at my wit's end. I won't have him moping around. He needs a job. I'm thinking, maybe you can get him in the union. It won't hurt to talk with Steve. He can carry nails, polish hammers, whatever. It's chicken, what does it look like? She yells, Jesus Henry Christ, it's supper time! Get out here! She looks at her husband. Talk to him, please. But does Joseph say anything? No, he just sits there, scarfing his food like an animal, his jaw clicking with every bite. Won't close his mouth when he chews. One day he's really going to piss her off, and she's going to tell him the truth, the whole truth, the immaculate truth.

# How the Boy Jesus Resisted Taking out the Trash

O there's not enough to bother with.

O in a couple thousand years the landfills will be groaning.

O we're too poor there isn't any trash.

O what about Naomi what does she do around here.

O if ever you suspected what's to come you'd put me in the best chair,
   you'd kill the last kid for supper and feed me the heart and the
   liver.

O not now.

O remember my father's business and all that. Priests and Levites are
   going to love me, some. Locusts will sing and sizzle. Precious
   stones will roll toward me like mice. Everybody's pretty
   daughters will cry because I don't like them that way.

O I'll change it into figs and honey later, all right?

O all right.

# The Carpenter

*Then Joseph being raised from sleep did*
*as the angel of the Lord had bidden him,*
*and took unto him his wife: And knew her not*
*till she had brought forth her first born son . . .*
—Matthew 1:24–25

*Someone* nailed her; and someone
would have to marry her, who
yet maintained she was a virgin—

mercy!—what with her belly bulging
like barrel staves. Still she was
a cutie: her bright eyes shining

like varnished mahogany, her skin
golden as honey oak. Finally, I spoke
plainly to her, as befits a man

of my trade, saying, "Sweetie,
you have snapped a chalk line
down the center of my heart,

cut through it cleanly; won't you
finish your work and be my wife?"
Which was a hard row from the git-go,

what with taxes and the necessary
commuting to construction sites;
plus there were the predictable

sniggers and jokes about another
man's chisel in my toolbox . . . .
But we managed. We survived.

And when the child arrived I
raised him as if he were my own,
instructed him in the many things

a carpenter should know: first
and last, good wood from bad;
how there's a time to sand

and a time to caulk; the wisdom
of working *with* the grain;
that every job must stop. Sad

to say, his aptitude was minimal,
his interest in the family business
nil. Instead, he read, brooded,

roamed the wilderness alone—
a sensitive boy, and bright, but
looking for god-knows-what. I don't.

Frankly, it worried the wife awhile.
Frankly, it worried me too. Though
isn't that just the way of the young.

Needing to figure it out on their own,
anything beating the old man's shoes?
Times were changing fast, it's true:

timber was scarcer; money tight. So
why not a future in fasting and prayer?
No chip off this block, the kid could be right.

# Inspiration

A mad girl dies bearing a bastard son
Who, instead of being left to starve,
Is trained by her uncle to work with wood.

By 10, the boy is muttering to the desert air,
Fouling his clothes, telling strangers,
"Bow down. I'm King David's heir." Still,

His intricate designs sell so briskly
His uncle tolerates his "eccentricities."
A year after the uncle dies, the "boy"—

Now thirty-three—is jailed for vagrancy.
Sentenced to death, he hears God whispering,
"My son," and tells his cell-mates, who rape him,

Jeering, "Smash this jail like Jericho,
And set us free!" He tries, beseeching God,
Battering the walls with his bare fists.

The next day he's crucified as he shrieks
God's vengeance down. Joking and laughing,
Roman soldiers raise his cross exactly

As an earthquake hits. Houses fall flat.
Corpses leap out of their graves as if
The earth has spit them back. Dust blocks the sun.

The carpenter dies raving. But one witness,
Matthew the Storyteller, sets to work.
Judas, who owes him money, makes the perfect

Villain in his tale. He throws in virgin
Birth, a star above a manger, wise men,
A holy child, as well as miracles,

Including one (since he has only
A crust and half a rancid herring in the house)
Where the wood-worker turns water

To wine, feeds a crowd with one fish
And a crust of bread, then speaks Matthew's own
Thoughts on heaven, sin, faith, treating

Others as you'd like them to treat you.
Friends make him tell his story again and again.
"It's your best work. Truly inspired," they say.

# Going Steady with Jesus

*(sung to a reggae beat)*

When he      asked me out
I was      afraid to go
Weird repu      tation
But I just couldn't say no
Goin      steady with Jesus
Goin      steady with he
Going      steady with Jesus
He's the only      boy for me

No one      knows how old
He never      held a job
Just go round      with the guys
Talking bout fishin and God
Going      steady with Jesus
Going      steady with he
Going      steady with Jesus
He's the only      boy for me

Tan like      the desert
He got      the gift of tongues

Wine give him          fire

Fasting keep him young

Going          steady with Jesus

Going          steady with he

Going          steady with Jesus

He's the only          boy for me


Only          just last Friday

He said          go steady with me

Promised          to love him

Love him          Eternally

Going          steady with Jesus

Going          steady with he

Going          steady with Jesus

Love him          Eternally

He's the only only boy for me!

# In Siena, Prospero Reconsiders the Marriage at Cana

All sleight-of-hand trails the dross and clutter
Of the unseen, clumsily like an anchor,
Barely concealing its means as it deceives.

What else can be made of signs and wonders
But close readings and a display of awe?
What is left when the wait-upon is fulfilled?

After the standoff Jesus conjures a trick.
Should such an act be enacted knowing
The next and the next will be demanded?

Of course, he one-ups himself, causes a fuss,
And the story plunges headlong to finale.
And then encore. Above, in the Sienese heat,

A pair of ravens patrol the parapet.
Washed linens flap on the clothesline.
A shadow bisects the curved blade of the Campo.

As if in confirmation of a miracle,

The twisted olive bears the wind's history,

A gnarl that hinders the brisk disorder,

Renders it as the unmoved here and now.

Skittish pigeons clatter up in the air.

Into shadow. Out of shadow. And then back down.

And no one, not even God, lifted a finger.

# What Are the Days?

They are pilferers
stealing our resolve,
Thomas broods aloud.

Or stones
to use for good or ill,
says James sitting
on a rock with Peter.

Soon, Jesus
comes along saying:
all days are brothers.

Aren't days fish
swimming to shore?
asks Simon, the fisherman
mending his nets.

They are coins to hoard
or to spend, Judas frowns,
and looks at his palms.

Twaddle, says Martha
running to fix supper.
You talkers, get me a hen,
get me an egg.

I bet you think
all the days are women
pouring wine and honey.

They are what they are,
says the hammerer of nails,
securing thieves
and Jesus to the cross,
nothing more.

# How the Other Thief Got into Heaven

When Jesus got back to heaven, the thief
to whom he had promised Paradise
when they were up on the cross
was already there. But the candelabra
that had stood on either side of the mantel
downstairs in the throne room
were missing. So were Jehovah's gold pocket-watch
& his silver cigar box,
the one that when you lifted the lid
played Handel's Messiah. Oddly enough,
the thief attempted neither to run nor to hide,
but was unconcernedly down on his knees in the chapel
piously praying. Accused, he owned up at once.
—Well, of course! He explained. For someone like me.
what else could Paradise mean but heavy gold
& windows with cheap locks.
But—but those things have been in the family for eons—
why, almost forever! Jesus exclaimed,
momentarily flustered and shaking his head,
Why, you can't—I mean—the very idea—
Okay, okay already, the other one answered. Look,

if you want I should give up my calling, consider it done.

But if you're asking me to get the swag back,

you can forget it. It's out of the question.

I mean there are middlemen, fences . . . Believe me,

the guys who work for the syndicate don't make returns.

But they have to! Cried Jesus. You don't know

what the old man is like when he's riled!

Remember Gomorrah? The Flood? The Amalekite Kingdom?

Hmmm, mused the thief, suppose if my buddy

were up here to help me . . .

Your buddy?

Yeah. You remember, the guy they hammered up on the cross

to your left. Believe me,

this is just the sort of caper he could pull off.

So I'm thinking if he could be sent for . . .

Impossible! Jesus protested.

That fellow never believed nor repented!

Well, if that's how you feel, shrugged the thief,

suit yourself. I mean none of that stuff

was in cherry condition to start with . . .

But this is outrageous! Cried Jesus.

It's boldfaced extortion!

Loving thy neighbor's how I see it, snapped back the thief.

Me and my buddy we go back a long ways . . .

Oh for heaven's sake! Jesus threw up his hands

at which very instant the reprobate under discussion

suddenly popped out of nowhere

to find himself standing beside them,

unshaven & flushed & stinking more than a little of sulfur

but flashing a big toothless grin nonetheless.

Now, whether Jesus was really all that upset

or simply putting it on for appearance's sake,

is still much disputed by biblical scholars.

What isn't at issue, however, is that the two rogues,

reunited in heaven, started dancing around

in a frenzy of whoops & backslaps, high-fives & hollers,

as gleeful as if they had finally hit the perfecta.

As for the stuff he had heisted,

the thief slapped his forehead. Heaven forfend!

How foolish of me to've forgotten!

Why I do believe the loot is just where I left it,

right over here in the baptismal font

wrapped up in Jehovah's long-johns.

& fishing them out he handed back

every last item: wetter for sure, but apparently

no worse for wear—the antique watch still,

in fact, merrily ticking—so that Jehovah

upon his return the next evening,

had no idea whatsoever they'd ever been gone.

Though even without that you can be certain

the old man found no lack of reason

to work himself into a lather in which he proceeded

to pummel his world with eruptions & famine

& mayhem & plague & every which sort

of calamitous woe—in his usual manner.

# Questions at Christmas

Whether he was born in winter,
Whether he was crucified,
Lanced with pity by a soldier,
Whether the apostles lied,
I cannot say, we cannot know.
Around us, drifts of whiteness blow.

If he was love he is alive
Even in the deadest night.
Those who in his name contrive
To punish love, theirs is a blight
More desolate than winter fields.
Ask what love the story yields?

What love discerns us from our birth
If any love beneath these stars
Discerns the children of this earth?
Who is the mother of our years?
What is the meaning of our prayers?
What love as certain as our fears?

# CONTEMPORARY JESUS

SWEET JESUS

# Final Scrimmage

Jesus was born at half-time
In the great football game of history.

That's why we're all dressed as linebackers now;

Prepare for the Final Scrimmage!

# Jesus Plays Super Sega

You can imagine the look on my face when I found Jesus
sitting
in the lotus position,
in the middle of my living room,
playing
Super Sega.

"Jesus," I said,
"what are you doing here?"

Jesus said,
"Wait a minute."

# When Jesus Came to Skokie

He sat towards the back of the #97 Old Orchard bus, reluctant
about making eye contact with the Polish and Hispanic maids,
on their way to work, who would surely recognize His familiar
profile quicker than those Russian Jews or godless teenagers.

He wore a Sports Walkman that He bought on sale at Howard
Station Electronics before boarding the bus and listened to
an Amy Grant tape that the young African-American sales clerk
had insisted on giving to Him because, as the kid said, He

looked so much like Richard Gere. He took notes in His Mighty
Morphin Power Rangers note-pad with a pencil He had made
Himself, noting how the south side of Howard Street was Chicago,
but the north side was Evanston. He thought that gasoline was

expensive here as the bus passed a filling station on the corner
of Howard and Ridge, and how strange it was to see Bethesda
Hospital, just west of Western Avenue, was still closed after
all these years, considering all the sickness and death on earth.

It touched Him when the bus-driver stopped to pick up a man in a wheelchair at the corner of Oakton and Dodge, how the other passengers swiftly vacated the seats that flipped back and folded up to make room for the differently-abled man. Secretly, He

marveled at the hydraulics of the vehicle, the way the front end of the bus lowered, like a camel, so the man in the wheelchair could roll aboard with ease. At Oakton and McCormick, as the bus crossed out of Evanston and into Skokie, He noticed a decided

difference in the air pressure, as if all the women on their way to cleaning houses had drawn in one collective breath of dread and refused to let it out, suffocation being preferable to servitude. He really expected to see tumbleweeds blowing through the deserted,

ghost-town streets of downtown Skokie and was more than a little relieved to see the brick and stained-glass majesty of St. Peter's church, where Lincoln Avenue and Niles Center Road split. He smiled to Himself, to think that He couldn't have better planned

the placement of Carson's Ribs directly across the street from
the Temple Judea reformed congregation. The Dempster
Skokie Swift depot looked markedly different from the last time He
had been to Skokie so He jotted a quick note about it along with

a commendation to the architect. A Chrysler with the vanity license
plate, MRS KIM, pulled alongside the bus, at the stop light near
the intersection of Church Street and Skokie Boulevard, and He could make
out a bumper sticker that said, "In Case Of Rapture, This Vehicle

Will Be Unattended." He shook His head, thinking to Himself,
don't be so sure. It was then that He realized that He'd forgotten
the receipt for the sandals He'd planned to exchange
for a different color in a larger size at Marshall Field's.

# Arrival

When Christ came back
no one was prepared, not even Aunt Sally,
a hardened Baptist who had the good grace
to witness Christ slide down a chute of light

onto her swimming pool. He stepped
across, knocked politely at the kitchen door.
Sally's mouth swung open. She'd been snapping
beans, a bushelful she'd bought at the farmer's

market that morning. The canning jars rattled,
boiling on the stove. Christ pointed to his Timex,
tapped the crystal. *Je-je-just a minute,* Sally
stammered, reeling in the kitchen, switching off

the stove. She yanked at her apron. Should she leave
a note for Bob? *Excuse me?* Christ said, his voice
like grainy honey. Sally whirled, surprised to find
her body slumped among the beans.

# Sunset, Route 90, Brewster County, Texas

Now the light is brass and pewter, alloyed metals solid as amber, allied with water,
umber and charnel, lucent as mercury, fugitive silver, chalk-rose and coal-blue, true,
full of the skulls and skeletons of moon light, ash light and furnace light, West Texas
whiskey light, bevel light, cusp light, light fall of arches and architectonics, earth
light and anchor light, sermon light, gospel light, light that clasps hands with the few
and the many, mesa light, salt bush and longhorn light, barbed wire and freight train
light, light of the suffering, light of the dusk-fallen, weal light and solace light, grave-
yard at the crossroads light, flood light, harbor light, light of the windmills and light
of the hills, light that starts the dove from the thistle, light that leads the horses to
water, light of the boon and bounty of the Pecos, light of the Christ of Alpine, light
of the savior of Marathon, Jesus of cottonwood, Jesus of oil, Jesus of jackrabbits, Jesus
of quail, Jesus of creosote, Jesus of slate, Jesus of solitude, Jesus of grace.

# Christians Killed My Jesus

Jesus was on his way to California
When he stumbled upon a marriage in the desert.
The party had just begun but they had run out of wine
and Jesus being Jesus
told them to bring out the empty carafes
and before their eyes geysers
of the best Chardonnay spewed forth and that as we know
is the miracle of the Chardonnay. And then and there
the newlyweds being astute entrepreneurs
signed him up to sell miracle wine
on the Internet and it seemed Jesus
was on his way to making it out West
but wait there's more when they found out
that he had multiplied bread in Boston
and fish in Maine and had made the snow-blind see
in Chicago and the arthritic walk
in Florida and had even been seen lifting the soul
of a battered boy somewhere in Montana
they said wait a minute there's more
to this motherfucker than meets the eye
and they emptied his pockets and found

a piece of the Dead Sea Scrolls and a lock
of John the Beloved's hair and on his palms
the hennaed tattoos of forgotten Bedouins
And underneath his eyelids       the remaining
Visions of the fatal Essenes and they x-rayed him
and tested his blood and they found in his veins
the last shrapnel of human love and
all our nostalgia and all our non sequiturs
and finally they said       listen Jesus
you carry a torch for the world
you're worth a lot of silver
but we just got to know have you or have you not
slept with a man have you or have you not
slit open an unborn child are you a fag
are you a nigger are you a slope
are you a jew and Jesus replied Love
only Love is all and that didn't make a lot
of sense so they said too bad
we thought we had something going on here
and they gathered a mob and nailed him
to a windmill outside of Joshua Tree

State Park and it was January and by nightfall
they trudged back to their homes and ate dinner
and turned on the TV and some sat up all night
watching reruns and waiting
for the second coming.

# Twang

I saw Jesus in New Mexico
reeking of guano
selling chilies from the back of a cart
older now, with two kids
one a teenager with a criminal record
the other a ten-year-old
who listens to the silence each night
to see if God is there somewhere
swears sometimes he hears Him singing

Look after my Dad
and mom whose bones we left in the canyon
among the coyotes and the cacti
look after the blossoming sage
the secret of light
they keep in their roots
and after me, your ordinary angel

Jesus crossed the border
years ago The scars don't show
anymore He walks with a limp

to remind himself
he has two legs and one road
ahead of him
America is bigger than heaven
and harder to get into
I'd like a piece of it anyway
and I pray so much
even prayer hurts my soul

Look after the boy who runs
amuck along the river
and the river with its fool's gold
and the throat of the gold
that produces its song
and the song like the ash of a cloud
still warm with thunder
and the thunder as it falls to its death
and me among the dry semillas
of the desolate arroyo

There's a rio grande
that cuts through my guts
get out of the way
sometimes I can almost touch
the edge and Big Bang of heaven
once though I wasn't drunk
I even heard it call my name

# Transplant

Good Friday, Christ entered L.A. County Medical
complaining of starvation and thirst.
He carried an orange parrot in a cage,
and hung on with both fists
even when the orderly
explained about straitjackets.
"It's my human soul," Christ shrieked.

The doctors consulted: his parrot
was the picture of health,
but Christ was on his last legs
and had to be completely rebuilt.

Transplants were invited:
throat, neck and skull from a priest
dead of cancer of the penis.
Strong back, arms and legs
from a lumberjack with alchoholic jaundice.
From a breathless starlet,
torso and internal organs.

When it came to the brain, they were stumped.
No donor came forward. The doctors
seized as one upon the parrot.

They stuffed the parrot's little brain
into the big skull, closed Christ up,
sent him to recovery.

Sunday morning, Christ woke up whole,
improved. He said, "Polly want a wafer,"
and flapped his lumberjack arms,
where the first orange feather sprouted.

# Love That Man Jesus

Jesus and I in a blue jeep. His hair
strokes the wind. Long hair. White teeth.
Sex incarnate. Let's say we're speeding
down a hill in Pittsburgh, PA.
Sandal to the floor, Jesus laughs.
*It's allright, Girl, you're with me.*

The neighbors think he's on drugs. My husband's
at Joe Bravo's filing for divorce. But Jesus
how can I say *no* when you're so gentle?
Jesus in my living room smoking
a cheroot. Jesus in blue denim stands at my stove
stirring lentil soup. Jesus in my bedroom
healing hands upon my sides.

Jesus calling from a phone booth in Cleveland,
Tennessee. He's transubstantiated live
at The Holy Angels Church. He says, *Girl,*
*you should have seen their faces when I did*
*the two-step down those marble stairs and sang*
*how love beats incense and claret wine.*

# Christ Riding

When I see Him walking, my foot
lifts off the gas. Turn signal on,
braking, skidding, I throw open the door. *Need a lift?*
He's wearing a white robe and sandals. No surprise.
His eyes touch mine and we're off,
windows down, hair blowing,
no safety belts. We believe in miracles.
In the country things haven't changed much.
A herd of cows, a couple of bulls,
corn growing high. We're going 65
and Rod Stewart croons *I love you* on FM
while an 18 wheeler barrels down on us.
Christ's nature is to smile but fumes from the truck
and trash flowering on the roadside
darken the light around us.
Near Harper's Lake, He raises His hand and I stop.
Jumping out, He stubs divine toe on rusty can,
then without a word walks onto the water,
all the way to the pier by Ginger's Cafe
where He turns and I hear
his voice clear above the lake.
*This old heart of mine, been broke a thousand times.*

# Poem from a Matchbook Cover

*Talk to Jesus*
*Dial 1 900 His Love*
*3.95 the first minute*
*1.95 each minute thereafter*

He's finally done it,
become the millionaire
we knew he'd be
way back in Nazareth.
Even as a kid
he could sell it,
took his daddy's
scraps of wood
to build a little pulpit
and stood in the market place
preaching and passing the plate.
We knew he was big
when he got to the city
on that donkey, the multitudes
and palm leaves and all,
but then they got him
on that tax evasion thing
and something about fraud,

the Jerusalem tabloids
having a field day
with those pictures of him
and that Magdalene chick,
and him tacked up on that cross
yelling the whole time
that they were, "just friends."

Took a miracle
to come back from that.
But now his love
comes recorded 24/7
off a switchboard
manned by 30 operators
workin' a storefront
in El Segundo.
And he's not doing that robe
and sandals bit anymore,
got his silk track suit
and a white stretch limo
parked at the studio
where he's cutting
one of those infomercial deals.

And why not?
We need him now more than ever,
all of us sinners
who sit in the dark
facing a flickering blue screen,
afraid
and not knowing what's worse,
the night
with its slow grip in the chest
or the phone bill
that's headed our way
in the mail.

# Jesus Tries to Get into the Movies

He figures it would be a
way to spread the word and get
close to some cool flashy
babes, but doesn't
understand when they tell
him he better get into
some union, he's been there,
done it, got the shirt he starts
to say but sees them looking
down at his ragged sandals as if
they were into feet. He doesn't
want to seem preachy, watches
a woman with a gold cross humming
"In the Beauty of the Lilies,"
walks up to ask if she knows
about salvation and she points
to this kettle out on the street
with a man in a military
uniform ringing a bell, looking
bonkers. If I'd have come back
earlier, Jesus thinks, maybe I could
have been in the story of my life.

Then he smiles, a little wryly.
When the casting director says,
looking down at his application
and seeing Jesus, "We had Willem
Dafoe and before him, Charlton
Heston. I'm afraid you're
not in their league. If you could
sing and dance, maybe we'd call,
down the road, in the next
century, for a bit part in a remake
of Superstar. Maybe an extra, though
pal, the way you come in here,
dressed in those hippy clothes—you
might call central casting, see if
they've got anything still not in the
can about unrest, student rioting—
maybe a Janis Joplin remake—you could
play a homicidal druggie, a nut seeing
what no one else does—you'd be ok
for something—a documentary on
happenings, the Love Generation.

# The Night of the Living Dead

Like a parasitic insect, stealthy Jesus
lays his eggs at the base of their skulls
and they hatch, raven through
the medulla, cerebellum and
the cerebrum: they are "saved,"
they are "blissful," they are
"born again." They wear galoshes,
they have sex only for procreation,
they are unemployed, they are
bound for glory because
they know one thing
(the only thing to know)
and they want to give it to you.
They are gathered this evening
before your door to offer tracts,
they are restrained, they don't
like to touch themselves, they
are standing here today quietly
though they burned Jews, though they
stoned heretics, though they inserted
flaming pokers into the anuses

of homosexuals. They're restrained, they
know God, they would like to tear
your arms from your sockets, they
are waiting until the world is dark enough
to tear the flesh from your thighs.

# What Happens in the Dark

The year will be the usual rewinding of the film
of the past and starting all over, but you can't see
the same film again without something being different.
When my older brother, the neighbors, and other strangers
bought snowblowers that summer after the biggest winter
since the nineteenth century,
it was easy to predict mild weather for the next winter.
And it came about that it snowed very little.

August comes and goes without the end of the world,
August being the most popular month for that in fiction,
but when the world does end, who will care what month it is?
Some believe that Jesus will come back in August,
but would we notice any difference when
there's an apocalypse every day?
The squirrel races itself across the street and up the tree.

My older brother develops a spur on his spine, goes
through physical therapy for five weeks, and is told
he should exercise his back every day for the rest
of his life to build up the muscles around the spur,
to avoid any recurrence of pain.

The depression of February is only momentarily distracted
by backaches, colds, the hearts and dark red roses
of Saint Valentine's Day, the celebration of love.
If the world ends in February chances are the last afternoon
will be dismal and grey, a dead cat on the side
of the road on the way home from the office.

My older brother never complains.
My mother says nothing ever bothers him, he's happy-go-lucky.
My younger brother became a father last year.
My mother says his son is a lot like me when I was a baby.
My older brother became a grandfather last year.
It doesn't bother him at all.

My father finally got new tires on his Ford truck.
Though he hasn't said so, I know he doesn't
approve of my Nissan sport-utility.
Is it more important to have a sexy set of wheels
than to know where you're going?

The beginning of spring is a month away.
Some say the son of God was born and died in April,
and Easter rabbits gathered around the manger
and the cross to adore the baby Jesus, the dying Jesus.
There is no way to prove any of this.

BRUCE BEASLEY

# *from* **Negatives of O'Connor and Serrano**

> . . . *writers who see by the light of their Christian faith will have, in these times the sharpest eyes for the grotesque, for the perverse, for the unacceptable.*
> —Flannery O'Connor

> *God created the body for a reason, and we were meant to exploit it.*
> —Andres Serrano

> *O one, on none, o no one, o you:*
> *Where did the way lead when it led nowhere?*
> —Paul Celan

*Negative 1*

Andres Serrano would jack off on Jesus

(the congressman said)

if the NEA would pay him to do it—

*What this Serrano fellow did,*

*he filled a bottle with his own urine*

*and stuck a crucifix down there,*

*he is not an artist, he is a jerk—*

—He jerks off

in the air, and photographs
his semen's fretted
transit through space, *Ejaculate*

*in Trajectory,* abjected seed. What leaves
the body. It's substance
he wants, not representation:
blood and cum, milk and Christ, submersible
icons. Black spume all around the Last Supper.
In O'Connor's *bleeding, stinking, mad*
*shadow of Jesus,* cibachrome
Pietá in cow's blood, Jesus seethed in piss—

Strip of negatives, images
stripped down to their substance, stripped of their light.

*Negative 8*

White Christ
purified in a vat of milk.

Hazel Motes: *One Jesus is as bad as another.*

Negatives, darkened texts,
reversed icons, blotched, from which
the representational illusion proceeds, print, and print—

*Of neither the things that are, nor of the things that are not*

From his butcher on 38th, Serrano
hauls back to the studio his gallons of blood

*Neither does He live, nor is He life*

In a dream, even books
are mortal: crusted
tumors on their pages, leeching
fleshwounds on their covers

*Neither can reason attain to Him, nor name Him, nor know Him*

(Serrano's
slammed and jeweled cathedral gates)

Hazel Motes: *Where
has the blood you think
you been redeemed by*


*touched you?*

# Straw Hat Jesus

sittin on the world,

legs swingin slow, heart unfurled

with robin-fat grace

of robin's breast orange,

hovering over, covering

our sparrow-size woe.


Straw hat Jesus leanin real low,

with your robin-head tilt

and robin-head stillness,

listening for the worm of our longing.


Straw hat Jesus when will we know,

that the wolves of our hunger,

driven thru the day,

at night find their den

in the curve of your arm.

# Lorna Sue Cantrell, Singing in the Choir

Jesus was my first lover
and the best. Oh, not
that Jesus hanging back of
the altar—that one's all
skim milk and Wonder Bread,
nothing to Him. I mean the Jesus
preacher told about the summer
I was fourteen: Jesus chasing
out the money changers. I'd spent
that summer shedding my cocoon
of baby fat, nerves scurrying
lizard-like beneath my skin,
and preacher's voice came thundering
down the aisles, while I sat,
mouth agape, and let it sweep
me on. I saw Him rampaging
through the temple, swinging whips
to drive out sinner, the sinews
on His arms and legs standing up
like tree roots, His eyes striking
sparks where they lit. I saw

His fingers tighten on the handle,
knuckles raised, and I thought
of how it'd be to feel
those hands on me, to hear
that voice stripping me bare
and laying me out with nothing
left to hide me from His eyes.
At the end, I let them carry
me up front and, gulping tears
like wine, I gave myself to
Him. That night, I lay spread-
eagled on my bed, while the Holy
Ghost probed every part of me,
feeling those carpenter's hands
reach inside me and twist till
something knotted there came loose,
and I cried, "Yes, Lord! Yes,
Lord! Lord, yes, yes!" jerking
like a catfish on a line. I never
had a man could match Him, never,
and before I married Raymond, I
tried plenty.

Sundays now, singing in the choir,
I don't see Him dangling from the cross.
I've never liked that ending
anyway. Meek is what I am
at home, Wednesday and Saturday nights,
while Raymond does his old one-two,
and I stare at the water stains,
wondering how I'll fix my hair
for work tomorrow. I don't want meek
here. It's up here in the choir I feel
my bones go soft inside, feel my skin
give off sparks like something wired,
while every pore spreads itself
for Jesus to come in. He's no
lamb, like preacher says, no gelded
sacrifice. Not Him. "Oh, Lamb
of God," the others whine, but I sing,
bold and strong. "Oh, Ram of God,"
I sing. "I come. I come."

# Why Jesus Ate in Bars

*—for Papa Jim Carone*

First of all, they have good food—
like at Papa's where from 5-10 Monday-Thursday
you can get homemade spaghetti and meatballs
all you can eat for $3.50.
Some patrons started calling it depression spaghetti
after the steel mill closed
and left half the town unemployed,
but Papa don't care what you call it.
"People gotta eat, don't they?" he says.

Then there's the drink.
On Fridays it's happy hour from 4-7
and free chicken wings (all you can eat)
with draft beer at 40 cents a glass.
You can afford to get boozed up
and don't have to remember
how your little town's going to pot.
Papa says, "Drink to enjoy; drink to forget.
Can't let people go thirsty, can we?"

Finally, there's the patrons;
Crazy Joe, who downs ten or twelve drafts
then tells anybody who'll listen
how the school took his house,
eminent domain cost him everything
tryin' to save it, went to eleven lawyers
at 75 bucks an hour.

At the beginning Joe said he'd shoot
the first son of a bitch who set foot on his property
be waitin' for 'em on the front porch with a shotgun
til the State Police showed up and he went peacefully.

There's Judy, who's got stomach trouble
drinks dinner, whines to the table next to her
about that lard-ass son she's supporting—
over 300 pounds, so fat he can hardly waddle
been unemployed long before the steel mill
ever thought of closing.

There's also Lance, just turned 21,

who staggers 'round the joint after nine or ten beers

feeds quarters to the juke box

puts his arm around anybody who doesn't mind his breath,

talks right in their face. Lance likes everybody,

thinks Jesus is the coolest dude he's ever met,

digs the long hair, sandals, gleam in his eyes.

He sits at Jesus's table and talks for hours

late when the bar empties out and nobody much is left.

Around 2, Papa yells "LAST CALL," sets down a couple brews.

He smiles at Lance, Jesus. Papa knows how everybody needs a

friend.

# Jesus at the Laundromat

The last crystals from the box of All
spill into the Speed Queen.
Tube socks, cotton drawers
with an asterisk design in blue,
a few frayed robes, graying now,
a sweatshirt saying GOD IS LOVE.
Jesus loads his quarters
and eases into a plastic chair
by the Change machine.
Each year it's harder to remember
why he returned.
Sometimes he knows
it was only nostalgia, and not
a second chance for anyone. Now
he longs for home. In heaven
things stayed white.
No one had to suffer fluorescent lights
or rattling dryers,
the sour pool of urine by the pay phone.
Jesus watches his clothes revolve,
suds hitting the surface

of the curved glass. He sighs

and looks around,

surprised he's not alone.

The chairs are filled

with old bodies, some snoring,

some sitting so still

he's tempted to touch them.

A woman curls under newspaper

near the sign that reads OPEN.

The attendant drags a mop

the length of the linoleum,

streaking the dirt.

LOAD CLOTHES EVENLY.

DO NOT DYE IN THESE MACHINES.

24 HOURS A DAY.

WASH 'N SAVE.

# Jesus at the A&P

buys Kitty Care litter,
Kosher pickles and canned black olives,
Top Ramen with whole wheat noodles,
a loaf of Roman Meal that will last him for weeks.
By the frozen foods he pauses
at the rows of TV dinners, and chooses
Benihana's Oriental Vegetables and Rice.
He passes up the fresh fish,
stranded on crushed ice, their filmed eyes
multiplied the length of the display case.
Now the girl in the Express lane
punching up his purchases, LILY
printed on a small gold pin
fastened to her tight tan uniform,
Lily of the dyed-purple bangs and gold
glitter eyelids, patterned pink stockings,
drops the pickles and curses—
*Christ*—and for a moment
the old guy's blurred eyes burn
and he sees right down to her bored
exhausted soul. But she looks

past him, severe and cold,

and calls a boy to fetch another jar.

Then Jesus hoists his plastic bags;

the automatic doors part, and he shuffles slowly out.

It's 5 o'clock and damp,

a long walk from here to his hotel room

on a dirty trash-filled street.

His hands and feet ache, his heart

feels tight. The lights of the parking lot

glow with little haloes in the mist.

# Jesus in the Nursing Home

refuses to speak.
He eats his pear Jell-O,
stares at the yellow liquid
pooling on the floor under his wheelchair.
Strapped in,
sliding anyway, he won't call
for help. The others don't notice.
*Dear God*, one says suddenly,
head snapping up and dropping
to one side. Jesus slides lower
and an aide hoists him up.
Most days he sits studying
the plastic cross
on the nail above his door,
trying to remember
something important. At night
there's the sound of someone laughing
down the bright white halls.
Today he's wheeled into the room
with the organ, where a girl
plays once a month. Her brother

sings hymns, and always ends
with When the Saints Go Marching In.
Some people tap time on their footrests.
Most of them watch the TV,
waiting for the screen to light up.
An aide hands out kazoos
they hold in their laps.
Jesus looks at the small instrument,
brings it to his lips and doesn't play.

# Jesus in Death

is small and bony in his blue pajamas.

His nightlight of Mary

glows on the bureau,

her eyes turned inward.

The nurses' shoes

pass by his room all night,

shushing and squeaking.

No one notices the throbbing light

under the door.

The dayshift finds the covers

thrown back, an empty bed.

Nothing on the pillow

but a handful of ashes.

A nurse brushes the pillows

and the grey flakes float up.

She crosses her arms.

An old woman weeps in the doorway,

then opens her bathrobe

and squats on the floor to shit.

*He must be somewhere,*

the nurse says. *Where are you?*

she calls, walking through the halls.

*Here,* come the voices

from every room.

*Here I am, here I am, here,*

*here, here.*

# Biographical Notes

**KIM ADDONIZIO** is the author of the poetry collections *The Philosopher's Club, Jimmy & Rita* and *Tell Me*, a Finalist for the National Book Award, and a book of short stories, *In the Box Called Pleasure*. With Dorianne Laux, she co-authored *The Poet's Companion: A Guide to the Pleasures of Writing Poetry*. She has received two NEA Fellowships. She is online at http://addonizio.home.mindspring.com.

**SHERMAN ALEXIE** is a poet, filmmaker and novelist. In 1992, Alexie received a National Endowment for the Arts Poetry Fellowship, and his first book, *The Business of Fancydancing*, was selected by the *New York Times Book Review* as a "Notable Book of the Year." Alexie's most recent book of poems is *One Stick Song* (Hanging Loose Press, 2000). He lives in Seattle, Washington, with his wife and two sons.

**REBECCA BAGGETT** is the author of two chapbooks, *Still Life With Children* and *Rebecca Baggett: Greatest Hits 1981-2000*, both from Pudding House Publications. Her poems, stories and essays appear in numerous journals and anthologies. She lives in Athens, Georgia, with her husband and two daughters.

**LYNNE BARRETT** is the author of two story collections, *The Secret Names of Women* and *The Land of Go* (both Carnegie Mellon University Press). She has won the Edgar Award for Best Mystery Story and has received an NEA Fellowship. She lives in Miami, Florida.

**BRUCE BEASLEY**'s latest book is *Signs and Abominations* (Wesleyan University Press, 2000). He won the 1993 Ohio State University Press/Journal Award for *The Creation* and the 1996 Colorado Prize (selected by Charles Wright) for *Summer Mystagogia*. He teaches at Western Washington University.

**LINDA BUTURIAN** writes short stories, essays and poetry, and lives in rural Minnesota with her husband and two daughters. Her work has appeared in such publications as the *Utne Reader* and *The Oregon Extension*. She was recently awarded a Blacklock Fellowship to work on her first novel.

**PHILIP DACEY** is the author of seven books of poetry, the latest *The Deathbed Playboy* (Eastern Washington University Press, 1999). His awards include two NEA Fellowships, a Woodrow Wilson Fellowship, three Pushcart Prizes, a Fulbright Lectureship in Yugoslavia, and a Quarterly Review of Literature Poetry Award.

**JIM DANIELS**' most recent books of poems include *Night With Drive-By Shooting Stars* (New Issues Press, 2002) and *Digger's Blues* (Adastra Press, 2002). His next collection of short stories, *Detroit Tales,* will be published by Michigan State University Press in 2003.

**JOHN DUFRESNE** is the author of the novels *Louisiana Power & Light*, *Love Warps the Mind a Little* and *Deep in the Shade of Paradise*.

**STEPHEN DUNN** is the author of twelve collections of poetry, including *Different Hours* (winner of the 2001 Pulitzer Prize) and the forthcoming *Local Visitations*, both from W.W. Norton. He is Distinguished Professor of Creative Writing at Richard Stockton College of New Jersey.

**NICK FLYNN**'s first book of poems, *Some Ether* (Graywolf Press, 2000), won the PEN/Joyce Osterweil Award and was a finalist for the *Los Angeles Times* Book Prize. His second collection, *Blind Huber* (also Graywolf Press), is due out in 2002. He was raised vaguely protestant in an Irish Catholic stronghold in Scituate, Massachusetts.

**STEPHEN FRECH** holds degrees from Northwestern University, Washington University in St. Louis and the University of Cincinnati. *Toward Evening and the Day Far Spent* won the Wick Poetry Chapbook Contest and was published by Kent State University Press. His second volume, *If Not For These Wrinkles of Darkness*, won the 2000 White Pine Press Poetry Prize.

**ERIC GAMALINDA** has published a book of poems, *Zero Gravity* (Alice James Books, 1999), which was awarded the Asian American Literary Prize in 2000. Born and raised in Manila, the Philippines, he currently lives in New York City and teaches at New York University.

**DAVID GRAHAM** has served as poetry editor of *Blue Moon Review* and has been Poet-in-Residence at the Robert Frost Place. He has had six collections of his poetry published, including *Second Wind* (Texas Tech, 1997), *Stutter Monk* (Flume, 2000) and *Magic Shows* (Cleveland State University Poetry Center, 1987). With Kate Sontag, he is co-editor of *After Confession: Poetry as Autobiography*. He is Professor of English at Ripon College.

**JEFF GUNDY**'s most recent books are *Rhapsody with Dark Matter* (poems) (Bottom Dog, 2000) and *Scattering Point: The World in a Mennonite Eye* (essays). He teaches at Bluffton College in Ohio. His work has appeared in *Georgia Review, Quarterly West, Shenandoah, Mid-American Review, Artful Dodge, Exquisite Corpse* and *North American Review,* among other journals.

**BARBARA HAMBY**'s second book, *The Alphabet of Desire*, won the 1998 NYU Prize for Poetry and was chosen by the New York Public Library as one of the twenty-five best books of 1999. A poem from the book appeared in *Best American Poetry 2000*. She teaches in the Creative Writing Program at Florida State University.

**MARY STEWART HAMMOND**'s poems have appeared in many magazines, including *The Atlantic, American Poetry Review, The New Yorker* and *The Paris Review*, and numerous anthologies. W.W. Norton published her prize-winning book *Out of Canaan*. Other awards include MacDowell and Yaddo fellowships. She teaches at the New York Writers Workshop.

**BARBARA HAUK** is a co-editor of *Pearl Magazine* and the author of *Confetti* (Event Horizon Press, 1993). She has had more than 100 poems printed in the small and academic presses. She has also written interviews and essays.

**JUDY HENDON**'s poems have appeared in a wide variety of journals. Her most recent work can be found in *Pearl* (as a featured poet), *Spillway* and *Blue Mesa Review*. She has taught workshops at Los Angeles County's Center for Creative Arts and now teaches English in Long Beach, California, where she lives with her family.

**DAVID HERNANDEZ**'s poems have appeared in *The Southern Review, Cream City Review, Quarterly West, Mississippi Review* and in the anthology *Another City: Writing from Los Angeles* (City Lights Books, 2001). His collections include *Man Climbs Out of Manhole* (Pearl Editions, 2000) and *Donating the Heart* (Pudding House Publications, 2001), which won the National Looking Glass Poetry Competition.

**TONY HOAGLAND** has published two collections of poetry: the first, *Donkey Gospel*, from Graywolf Press (1998) and the second, *Sweet Ruin*, from the University of Wisconsin Press (2000). Both are still in print. His third collection of poems will be published by Graywolf in 2003. He currently works at the University of Pittsburgh.

**ANDREW HUDGINS** has published five books of poetry, all with Houghton Mifflin: *Babylon in a Jar* (1998), *The Glass Hammer* (1995), *The Never-Ending* (1991), a finalist for the National Book Award in 1991, *After the Lost War* (1988), which received the Poets' Prize in 1989, and *Saints and Strangers* (1985), one of three finalists for the 1985 Pulitzer Prize in Poetry. He is also the author of a collection of literary essays, *The Glass Anvil* (University of Michigan Press, 1997). Hudgins is professor of English at Ohio State University.

**COLETTE INEZ** has authored eight collections of poetry, most recently *Clemency* (Carnegie Mellon University Press, 1998). She has received fellowships from the Guggenheim and Rockefeller Foundations, and two from the NEA. A visiting professor at Cornell, Ohio, Bucknell and Colgate Universities and at Kalamazoo College, she is currently on the faculty of Columbia University's Writing Program where she has taught since 1983.

**MARY KARR**'s poems and essays have won Pushcart Prizes and have appeared in such magazines as *The New Yorker*, *The Atlantic* and *Parnassus*. Her previous books of poetry are *Abacus*, *The Devil's Tour* and *Viper Rum*. Karr lives in Syracuse, New York, where she is the Jesse Trusdale Peck Professor of English Literature at Syracuse University.

**JULIA KASDORF** is the author of two collections of poetry, both published by the University of Pittsburgh Press: *Eve's Striptease* (1998) and *Sleeping Preacher* (1992), which won the Agnus Lunch Starret Prize and the Great Lakes Award for New Writing. She is Associate Professor of English at Pennsylvania State University where she directs the MFA program in Creative Writing. Pertinent to this anthology, she previously taught creative writing at Messiah College.

**HERB KITSON** teaches at the University of Pittsburgh at Titusville. He received an International Merit Award in the *Atlanta Review* 2001 Poetry Contest. Recent work has appeared in *Chiron Review, The Comstock Review, The Kit-Cat Review, Thorny Review* and in the "New Beat Poets" issue of *Nebo*.

**RON KOERTGE**, a teacher at Pasadena City College, is the author of many books of poems as well as novels for young adults. His latest collection of poetry is *Geography of the Forehead* (University of Arkansas Press, 2000), and his newest young-adult novel is called *Stoner & Spaz*, a title that causes librarians to quake in their boots.

**STEVE KOWIT**'s latest collection is *The Dumbbell Nebula* from Heyday Press. He is also the author of *In the Palm of Your Hand: The Poet's Portable Workshop* and is the recipient of an NEA, a Pushcart Prize and several other honors. He teaches at Southwestern College in San Diego, California.

**MAXINE KUMIN** is the author of thirteen books of poems, most recently *The Long Marriage*. In 1973, Kumin was awarded the Pulitzer Prize for *Up Country*, her fourth book of poems. She served as Consultant in Poetry to the Library of Congress before that post was renamed Poet Laureate Consultant of the United States, and as the Poet Laureate of New Hampshire from 1989 to 1994.

**GERRY LaFEMINA** is the author of *Zarathustra in Love* and *Shattered Hours: Poems 1988-94*, among other books; a new collection, *Graffiti Hear*, is forthcoming from Mammoth Books in 2003. He is also co-translator, with Sinan Toprak, of *Voice Lock Puppet*, a collection of poems by the contemporary Turkish poet Ali Yuce. He edits the journal *Controlled Burn* and lives in Morgantown, West Virginia.

**DORIANNE LAUX** is the author of three collections of poetry from BOA Editions: *Awake* (1990), introduced by Philip Levine, *What We Carry* (1994), a finalist for the National Book Critics Circle Award, and *Smoke* (2000). Among her awards are a Pushcart Prize for poetry, two fellowships from the NEA and a Guggenheim Fellowship. She teaches at the University of Oregon's Program in Creative Writing.

**LYN LIFSHIN**'s *Before It's Light,* published by Black Sparrow Press in 1999, won the Patterson Poetry Prize. *Cold Comfort* (Black Sparrow Press, 1997) will be reprinted in 2001. Black Sparrow will continue to publish a series of her books including *Blue Sheets* in 2002. Her Website is www.lynlifshin.com.

**TIMOTHY LIU** is the author of four books of poems, most recently *Hard Evidence* (Talisman House, 2001). He lives in Hoboken, New Jersey.

**MARK M. MARTIN** received his MFA in creative writing from Florida International University. His work has appeared in *Vox, Slipstream, Red Rock Review, New Millennium Writing* and *The Cream City Review*. He lives in Hollywood, Florida.

**CAMPBELL McGRATH** is the author of five books of poetry, most recently *Florida Poems* (Ecco Press, 2002). The recipient of a 1999 MacArthur Fellowship, he teaches in the Creative Writing Program at Florida International University in Miami.

**DAVID MASON**'s books include two prize-winning collections of poetry, *The Buried Houses* and *The Country I Remember*, both from Story Line Press. His collection of essays, *The Poetry of Life and the Life of Poetry*, appeared in 2000. He has also edited several anthologies. He teaches at Colorado College.

**SUSAN HERPORT METHVIN** is a graduate of Warren Wilson's MFA Program. She has had poems published in *Amaryllis*, *The Beloit Poetry Journal* and the online literary magazine *CRANIA*. Her poem "Breast Imaging" appears in *Art.Rage.Us: Art and Writing by Women with Breast Cancer* (Chronicle Books, 1998). Poems from *They Wrote Us A Poem IV* and *V* are on display at Duke Medical Center.

**RON MOHRING**'s first collection, *Amateur Grief*, won the 1998 Frank O'Hara Chapbook Award; a second, *Terra Infirma*, is forthcoming from Inleaf Press. His poems have appeared in *Artful Dodge*, *Bay Windows*, *Blue Moon Review*, *Green Mountains Review*, *Gettysburg Review*, *Hanging Loose*, *The Louisville Review* and other journals. He currently lives in Lewisburg, Pennsylvania, teaches at Bucknell University and is associate editor of *West Branch*.

**DAVID A. NEAL, JR**. lives in Tucson, Arizona, where he moved after early retirement. While living in Long Beach, California, he participated in workshops led by Donna Hilbert, Lisa Glatt, and in Tucson, one led by Will Inman. He has been published in *Black Cross*, *Chiron Review*, *Good News*, *Erete's Bloom* and *Laughing Dog*.

**ED OCHESTER** edits the Pitt Poetry Series and teaches in the MFA program at Bennington College. His most recent books are *The Land of Cockaigne* (Story Line Press, 2001) and *Snow White Horses: Selected Poems* (Autumn House Press, 2000). With Judith Vollmer, he edits the poetry magazine *5 AM*.

**JAMES O'KEEFE** has an MFA from the University of Maryland and a law degree from Harvard. He is pretty sure that both Nietzsche and God are dead. He lives in Maine with Margaret, Devlin and Edie—a trinity more snacktastic than any in the Big Book. James keeps a manuscript of poems, *Muscle*, entombed in a desk drawer. It is enough to make you cry.

**ERIC PANKEY** is the author of five collections of poetry: *For the New Year*, which won the Walt Whitman Award from the Academy of American Poets, *Heartwood*, *Apocrypha*, *The Late Romances* and *Cenotaph*. He is a professor of English at George Mason University.

**MOLLY PEACOCK** is Poet-in-Residence at the Cathedral of St. John the Divine in New York. Her most recent books are *Cornucopia: New & Selected Poems* (W.W. Norton, 2002) and *How To Read A Poem and Start A Poetry Circle* (Riverhead Books, 1999). Peacock is one of the creators of the Poetry in Motion series featured on the nation's subways and buses. She lives in Toronto and New York City.

**LUCIA PERILLO** has published three books of poetry, the most recent of these being *The Oldest Map With the Name America* (Random House, 1999). Her poetry, essays and short fiction have appeared in many magazines and have been reprinted in the *Pushcart* and *Best American Poetry* anthologies. In the year 2000 she received a MacArthur Fellowship for her writing. She lives in Olympia, Washington.

**LUIS J. RODRÍGUEZ** is the award-winning author of three poetry collections. He is also founder-director of Tia Chucha Press in Chicago and a co-founder of Tia Chucha's Cafe Cultura—a bookstore, coffee shop, art gallery and performance space in the Northeast San Fernando Valley section of Los Angeles.

**CATIE ROSEMURGY**'s first book of poetry, *My Favorite Apocalypse*, was published in 2001 by Graywolf Press. Her work has appeared in such journals as *Poetry Northwest*, *River Styx*, *Ploughshares* and *Best American Poetry*. She teaches creative writing at The College of New Jersey.

**THADDEUS RUTKOWSKI**'s novel *Roughhouse* (Kaya Press, 1999) was a finalist for the Members' Choice of the Asian American Literary Awards. His work has appeared in the book *The Outlaw Bible of American Poetry*, the journals *American Letters & Commentary* and *Fiction* and elsewhere. He has been trying to communicate with a higher power for several years now.

**MAUREEN SEATON** has won, among others, a National Endowment for the Arts Fellowship, two Pushcart Prizes, the Iowa Prize, the Lambda Book Award, and the McAfee Discovery Award for her books of poetry *Furious Cooking, The Sea among the Cupboards* and *Fear of Subways*. Her most recent book is entitled *Little Ice Age* (Invisible Cities Press, 2001).

**GREGG SHAPIRO**'s poetry and fiction have been published widely. He is the music and cinema editor at *Windy City Times* (Chicago) and the music editor at *Next Magazine* (New York). He is also a contributing writer to a variety of publications including *Bay Area Reporter, Between The Lines, En La Vida, Gay and Lesbian Times, Gay Life* and *Xtra!*, to name a few.

**PETER JAY SHIPPY** was born in Niagara Falls. He is a graduate of Emerson College and the Iowa Writers' Workshop. His poems and fiction have been published in such literary journals as *Epoch, The Harvard Review, Ploughshares* and *Poetry Ireland*. He has taught literature and creative writing at Emerson College since 1987.

**JIM SIMMERMAN** is the author of four full-length poetry collections, most recently *Kingdom Come* (Miami University Press, 1999), and is co-editor of *Dog Music: Poetry About Dogs* (St. Martin's Press, 1995). He lives in Flagstaff, Arizona, and is Professor of English at Northern Arizona University.

**HAL SIROWITZ** is the Poet Laureate of Queens, New York. He is the author of two collections of poems, *Mother Said* and *My Therapist Said*. *Mother Said* has been translated into nine languages, made into an animated film, adapted to the stage in Norway and put to music.

**SPARROW** writes a column ("Quarter to Three") for *Chronogram* (www.chronogram.com); he is art critic for *New Renaissance* (www.ru.org). He lives with his wife, Violet Snow, and Sylvia, his daughter, in the epiphanous Catskill Mountains of New York. His town is Phoenicia. His two books are *Republican Like Me* and *Yes, You ARE a Revolutionary*. His favorite color is Imperial Brown.

**DIANE SPODAREK**. Born in Canada, grew up in Detroit: founder and editor of *Detroit Artists Monthly*. Singer/guitar player with Dangerous Diane Band. NEA grant for video. New York: three NYFA fellowships. Recent theater gig: one-person show "The Drunk Monologues." Writing published in *Even More Monologues for Women by Wome*n. Lives on the Lower East Side in New York with her daughter Dana.

**STEVEN STYERS** has been published in magazines such as *The Humanist* and *West Branch* and the anthologies *Summer Shade*, *More Than Animals* and *American Poets Say Goodbye to the 20th Century*. He is the coordinator of the Writing Center at Bucknell University. He's a cat lover and a kite flyer.

**VIRGIL SUÁREZ** was born in Havana, Cuba, in 1962. Since 1974 he has lived and traveled extensively in the United States. His poetry titles include *Palm Crows*, *Banyan* and *Guide to the Blue Tongue*. He divides his time between Key Biscayne and Tallahassee, Florida, where he lives with his wife and daughters and is a professor of creative writing at Florida State University.

**JAMES TATE** is the author of thirteen books of poetry and is the recipient of numerous awards, including the National Book Award and the Pulitzer Prize. *Dreams of a Robot Dancing Bee* (Verse Press, 2001) is his most recent book and his first collection of fiction.

**JON TRIBBLE**'s poems have appeared in *Crazyhorse*, *Ploughshares*, *Poetry* and *Prairie Schooner*. His work was selected as the 2001 winner of the Campbell Corner Poetry Prize from Sarah Lawrence College. He teaches at Southern Illinois University at Carbondale, where he is the managing editor of the Crab Orchard Award Series in Poetry published by Southern Illinois University Press.

**JACK VEASEY**'s eighth book of poems, *The Moon in the Nest*, was published earlier this year by Crosstown Books. His poems and nonfiction have appeared in periodicals ranging from *Experimental Forest Magazine* to *The Philadelphia Inquirer*. He grew up Irish Catholic in Fishtown, a working class neighborhood in Philadelphia, and now lives near Harrisburg.

**STACEY WAITE**'s poems have been published most recently in *Chiron Review*, *Concrete Wolf*, *West Branch* and *5 AM*. Her work received second place for the 2001 Pearl Poetry Prize and for the 2002 Frank O'Hara Award. Born in New York, Waite is now living in Pittsburgh where she is currently a Visiting Lecturer in the English Department at the University of Pittsburgh.

**MICHAEL WATERS** teaches at Salisbury University on the Eastern Shore of Maryland. His most recent book is *Parthenopi: New and Selected Poems* (BOA Editions, 2001); he has co-edited *Contemporary American Poetry* (with the late A. Poulin, Jr.; Houghton Mifflin, 2001) and *Perfect in Their Art: Poems on Boxing from Homer to Ali* (with Robert Hedin; Southern Illinois University Press, 2003).

**CHARLES HARPER WEBB**'s fifth book of poems, *Tulip Farms and Leper Colonies*, was published in 2001 by BOA Editions. He has received the Morse Poetry Prize, the Tufts Discovery Award, the Pollak Prize, a Whiting Writer's Award and a Guggenheim Fellowship. He teaches at California State University, Long Beach.

**CRYSTAL WILLIAMS** is the author of *Kin* and *Lunatic*. Her work appears in journals and anthologies such as *Pleiades, The Crab Orchard Review, 5AM, Callaloo, Ms. Magazine* and *American Poetry: The Next Generation,* among others. She teaches at Reed College in Portland, Oregon.

# Acknowledgments

*The editors wish to give special thanks to Mia Pardo, Patrick Pardo, Rick Peabody, David Hernandez, Allison Joseph, Tony Hoagland and Dan Wakefield.*

Permission for the inclusion of the poems in this anthology has been graciously granted by the publishers and individuals indicated below.

Kim Addonizio: "Jesus at the Laundromat" from *Beloit Poetry Journal.* Reprinted by permission of the poet. "Jesus at the A&P," "Jesus in the Nursing Home" and "Jesus in Death" appear by permission of the poet.

Sherman Alexie: "Eucharist" appears by permission of the poet.

Rebecca Baggett: "Lorna Sue Cantrell Singing in the Choir" from *New England Review*. Reprinted by permission of the poet.

Lynne Barrett: "Going Steady with Jesus" appears by permission of the poet.

Bruce Beasley: Forty-four lines of "Negatives of O'Connor and Serrano" from *Signs and Abominations*. Copyright © 2000 by Bruce Beasley. Reprinted by permission of the poet and Wesleyan University Press. "The Cursing of the Fig Tree" appears by permission of the poet.

Linda Buturian: "Straw Hat Jesus" appears by permission of the poet.

Philip Dacey: "The Feet Man" appears by permission of the poet.

Mary Stewart Hammond: "Jesus Rum" from *Out of Canaan* by Mary Stewart Hammond. Copyright © 1991 by Mary Stewart Hammond. Reprinted by permission of W.W. Norton & Company, Inc.

Barbara Hauk: "Transplant" from *Confetti*, Event Horizon Press. Copyright © 1993 by Barbara Hauk. Reprinted by permission of the poet.

Judy Hendon: "Poem From a Matchbook Cover" appears by permission of the poet.

David Hernandez: "Gold Jesus" appears by permission of the poet.

Tony Hoagland: "Just Spring" appears by permission of the poet.

Andrew Hudgins: "Dead Christ" from *The Never-Ending* by Andrew Hudgins. Copyright © 1991 by Andrew Hudgins. Reprinted by permission of Houghton Mifflin Company. All rights reserved.

Colette Inez: "What Are the Days" from *Family Life*, Story Line Press. Copyright © 1988 by Colette Inez. Reprinted by permission of the poet.

Mary Karr: "Descending Theology: The Crucifixion" appears by permission of the poet.

Julia Kasdorf: "Uncle" from *Sleeping Preacher*. Copyright © 1992 by Julia Kasdorf. Reprinted by permission of the University of Pittsburgh Press.

Herb Kitson: "Why Jesus Ate in Bars" appears by permission of the poet.

Campbell McGrath: "Sunset, Route 90, Brewster County, Texas" from *American Noise* by Campbell McGrath. Copyright © 1994 by Campbell McGrath. Reprinted by permission of HarperCollins Publishers Inc. Ecco Press.

Susan Herport Methvin: "Love That Man Jesus" from *The Trees Are Mended*. Copyright © 1986 by Susan Herport Methvin. Reprinted by permission of Northwoods Press. "Christ Riding" appears by permission of the poet.

Ron Mohring: "Arrival" from *West Branch*. Copyright © 1995 by Ron Mohring. Reprinted by permission of the poet.

David A. Neal, Jr.: "Dear Ann" and "Born Again" appear by permission of the poet.

Ed Ochester: "The Night of the Living Dead" appears by permission of the poet.

James O'Keefe: "Divine Self-Determination" appears by permission of the poet.

Eric Pankey: "In Siena, Prospero Reconsiders the Marriage at Cana" from *The Late Romances: Poems* by Eric Pankey. Copyright © 1997 by Eric Pankey. Reprinted by permission of Alfred A. Knopf, a division of Random House, Inc.

Molly Peacock: "Simple" from *Original Love* by Molly Peacock. Copyright © 1995 by Molly Peacock. Reprinted by permission of W.W. Norton & Company, Inc.

Lucia Perillo: "Cranky Jesus," "Chubby Jesus" and "Lazy Jesus" appear by permission of the poet.

Virgil Suárez: "The Face of Jesús in Campbell's ABC Tomato Soup" appears by permission of the poet.

James Tate: "Goodtime Jesus" from *Selected Poems*. Copyright © 1991 by James Tate. Reprinted by permission of Wesleyan University Press.

Jon Tribble: "Kung Pao Christ" appears by permission of the poet.

Jack Veasey: "The Son of Man" appears by permission of the poet.

Stacey Waite: "Jesus is Hanging over the Lesbian" appears by permission of the poet.

Michael Waters: "Christ at the Apollo" from *Green Ash, Red Maple, Black Gum: Poems*. Copyright © 1990 by Michael Waters. Reprinted by permission of BOA Editions, Ltd.

Charles Harper Webb: "Inspiration" from *Prosodia*. Reprinted by permission of the poet.

Crystal Williams: "On Getting Happy" appears by permission of the poet.